BREAK IT UP

A Teacher's Guide to Managing Student Aggression

**Arnold P. Goldstein · James Palumbo
Susan Striepling · Anne Marie Voutsinas**

Research Press
2612 North Mattis Avenue
Champaign, Illinois 61821

Advisory Editor, Frederick H. Kanfer

5 4 3 2   98 99

Illustrations by Elizabeth Scholder
Cover design by Doug Burnett
Composition by Tradewinds Imaging
Printed by BookCrafters

ISBN 0–87822–351–7
Library of Congress Catalog Number 94–69915

DISCLAIMER

The techniques and information contained in chapter 3, "Physical Intervention," of this publication are not meant as a substitute for supervised training, instruction, or accreditation, and the completion or review of the information set forth in chapter 3 does not imply any type of certification or competency. The information in chapter 3 is meant for instructional purposes to be used in combination with other instructional tools under the guidance of an accredited teacher or instructor. The techniques discussed are used for illustration only, and there is no warranty or assertion that such techniques are appropriate in all circumstances. The publisher and the authors make no warranty of any kind, express or implied. User assumes all risk and liability resulting from the use of the techniques or information contained therein. The publisher and the authors neither assume nor authorize any person to assume for the publisher and the authors any other liability in connection with the sale or use of the techniques or information contained in this publication.

This publication provides step-by-step procedures

for safely handling student disruptiveness and aggression

as well as student fights.

The comprehensive fight management system

detailed in this publication

is demonstrated in the videotape

**Break It Up
Managing Student Fights**

available from Research Press.

To the American teacher

Contents

Tables

Introduction

As student aggression, disruptiveness, and disrespect have grown in American schools, as they apparently have to a marked degree in recent years, efforts aimed at better understanding, preventing, and remediating such behaviors have proliferated. This book, in fact, provides as an appendix an annotated reference list of 31 books, book chapters, and journals describing procedures teachers are likely to find useful in dealing with such in-school behaviors. Valuable as these writings may be, it is noteworthy that, whereas all of them are written *for* teachers, none is written *by* teachers. Teacher experience and wisdom regarding such student behaviors remain, to a large degree, grossly untapped resources. The present book seeks to help correct this situation.

Chapter 1 starts where all efforts to manage student aggression should begin, with prevention. We seek here to offer teacher perspectives on the characteristics of low-aggression classrooms, classrooms in which student aggression is an infrequent event. Such classrooms are noteworthy for their sense of "us," of community, concretized in age-appropriate ways; for the skilled manner in which classroom rules are framed and implemented; for the clarity and conduct of everyday classroom procedures; for the breadth and richness of home-school collaboration; and for safety-promoting physical arrangements. The nature and facilitation of these related themes are the substance of this chapter.

Chapter 2 is, in some ways, the teacher wisdom at the heart of this book. We gathered reports of 1,000 episodes of low-, mid-, or high-level student aggression and its management from teachers in eight geographically dispersed states. Elementary, middle, and senior high school teachers in urban, suburban, and rural school districts participated in this effort. Targets of this individual and collective aggression included other students, teachers, and other school personnel. In all, this incident pool proved to be an exceedingly rich

1

data base from which to draw. In this chapter, we report a large number of diverse incidents and describe both successful and unsuccessful tactics employed toward their resolution. We have titled this chapter "Aggressive Incidents and Their Lessons" and believe that significant aggression management lessons for the contemporary teacher have indeed been derived.

Both teachers and students appear to be increasingly vulnerable to physical injury in American schools. The so-called battered teacher syndrome is no longer a rare occurrence. In addition to its some-times serious psychological and physiological components, student aggression increasingly results in severe physical injury to teachers. In response to this threat, chapter 3 provides step-by-step instruc-tion, via text and illustration, in a full array of self-protection and student containment techniques useful in classroom and other school-based settings.

Finally, the appendix offers access to resources for the reader wishing further materials dealing in a highly practical manner with discipline, classroom management, student aggression, and school violence. The resources in this comprehensive annotated bibliography of "how-to" information are authored by academics, researchers, and similar professionals, and are included here to complement this book's primary information base, derived from classroom teachers themselves.

Prevention: The Low-Aggression Classroom

In focusing on "breaking it up," this book primarily targets low, moderate, and high levels of student aggression, in its diverse and increasingly frequent forms of expression. However, we would be remiss if we did not also address the prevention of such behavior. In the present chapter we seek not to provide an extended discussion of discipline and classroom management, about which a number of excellent resources already exist (see the appendix). Instead, our focus will be the organization, structure, and defining procedures, that in the collective experience of both our teacher interviewees and ourselves, typically characterize the low-aggression classroom.

The days of children sitting quietly with hands folded in front of them, waiting for the lesson to begin, are long gone. As we interviewed teachers and brainstormed among ourselves, we kept asking, Why do some teachers have aggression less frequently in their classrooms than others? Why do some teachers always seem to be sending students to the front office on a referral, while others rarely do? There are qualities successful classroom teachers seem to share. This does not mean that these teachers never have aggression problems in their classes. They do. But the aggressive incidents seem to be lower level, shorter, and less frequent. We believe a low-aggression climate enables these teachers to maintain order and provide a facilitative classroom in which learning can and does occur.

Prevention of aggression in the classroom begins long before the students step through the door the first day. It begins with the

3

teacher's thinking through, as clearly and concretely as possible, the classroom demographics, organization, and procedures that may influence the in-school behavior of the students to come. Included in this consideration are the composition of the class and class members' probable level of interpersonal and aggression control skill, the physical characteristics of the classroom, teaching plans, plans for classroom community building, rules and procedures governing student behavior, available rewards and sanctions for such behavior, and the nature of efforts directed toward facilitative home-school collaboration. Each of these concerns is relevant to the level of classroom aggression.

THE STUDENTS

Prevention begins with an understanding of the student population you will be teaching (i.e., numbers, gender, economic levels, cultural backgrounds, racial composition, special needs). If you are a new teacher this means spending time prior to the first day with someone in the building who can tell you about your class. If you are an experienced teacher and have been in the building even a year, you already have much of this information. Although the specific makeup of your classes changes each year, the overall population of the building does not. Novice or veteran, it will serve you well to learn in advance about students and situations likely to draw heavily upon your aggression management skills. We are keenly aware of the danger in this recommendation. For example, knowing in advance that a student received in-school suspensions eight times last term may function as an aggression-eliciting, self-fulfilling prophecy during your term with him or her. We feel this risk can be moderated, however, to the extent that you seek to discern for each student not only how to thwart or minimize disruptiveness or aggression but also how best to facilitate classroom learning and on-task behavior.

TEACHING PLANS AND INSTRUCTIONAL BEHAVIOR

The first weeks of school are among the most stressful of the school year. Everyone, teachers and students, is in a transition period, and change is difficult. Successful teachers anticipate this stressful time and do as much of their planning as possible for the first weeks of school before school opens. They organize not only their materials and supplies but also their classrooms, taking into consideration safety and academic needs. They do a general long-range outline and a very specific 2-week teaching plan, and they clearly articulate for themselves their intended classroom procedures before the first day of school. By being organized to this degree, they are better able to deal with the inevitable confusion, disruption, and even chaos that can occur as everyone learns new routines.

What do teachers actually *do* in low-aggression classrooms? Observations and interviews combined with the relevant research literature suggest a half-dozen particularly fruitful teacher behaviors.[1] First, the teacher in the low-aggression classroom knows what is going on. Such *with-it-ness* is communicated to the class by consistent and swift recognition and, if necessary, consequating of behaviors likely to lead to disruptiveness or more serious aggression. Closely connected to such attentiveness is *overlapping*, the ability to manage successfully two or more classroom events, be they instructional or disciplinary. *Smoothness*, the ability to transition without downtime from one classroom activity to the next, is a third facilitative teacher behavior. Downtime is a good time for boredom-engendered acting-out; avoiding or minimizing it significantly deters such behaviors. Another way to minimize boredom is by instructing with *momentum*, maintaining a steady sense of progress or movement throughout a particular lesson, class, or school day. A *group focus*, the ability to keep the entire class involved in a given instructional activity, also diminishes the likelihood of student aggression. When the teacher attends only to a subgroup of students, the remainder of the class is available for disruptiveness or mayhem. Finally, and, to us, an especially significant contributor to a low-aggression classroom, is the communication by the teacher of consistently optimistic *academic expectations*. Students live up to (and, unfortunately, also down to) what significant persons in their lives—such as teachers—expect of them. The teacher who expects a sixth grader to read at a third-grade level because of his or her past record, or a sibling's "slowness," or the neighborhood he or she came from will likely be rewarded with a third-grade performance. By contrast, the teacher who, in the wide variety of ways available to teachers, lets the student know he or she can achieve and will have the teacher's help along the way is likely to motivate the student to be more academically successful and less behaviorally disruptive. It does not stretch the point to assert, with regard to both academic performance and classroom comportment, that at times what significant others expect we can achieve is a potent impetus toward such achievement. Expect the best of your students—you may get it.

COMMUNITY BUILDING

Successful teachers, defined as those whose classroom aggression levels are very low and whose students achieve satisfactory academic gains, often spend considerable time in the first few weeks of school creating a community of learners in their classrooms. The time and effort spent working toward this goal differs at different school levels (elementary, middle, and high school), yet our interviews across levels suggest that in low-aggression classrooms there typically exists a climate of cooperation, collaboration, and respect for all learners, generated by both teacher and students. During the early days and weeks of the term, students and teachers in these classrooms participate in activities that promote the building of a sense of community, with curriculum being of secondary importance. To carry forward this effort, teachers and students learn and use one another's names, listen carefully to one another, and share information to discover likes, strengths, and similarities. As much as is feasible, activities involve the whole class. Such community-building activities can take form in preplanned games and simulations.[2]

These activities share the common goal of giving students the opportunity to get to know one another. When a new group comes together, as a "room" at the elementary level and as a "class" at the middle school and high school levels, initially they are a group of strangers. It takes time for a group identity to form. The goal of the low-aggression classroom should be to create a group identity based on cooperation rather than competition. This means that instead of an atmosphere in which students feel, "If I learn (and get an A) that means you will not learn (and fail or, at best, achieve less well)," the low-aggression classroom promotes the idea that all students can learn and help one another do well. It need not be a cooperative learning classroom for students to feel that "Your learning and doing well enhances me rather than takes away from me." Research on aggression has shown a number of times that the more empathy a person has, the less aggressive he or she is and vice versa—the more aggressive a person is, the less empathy he or she has. We believe that the creation of a community in the classroom through the use of community-building exercises, activities, and teaching procedures encourages empathy. In low-aggression classrooms, such teaching is often present.

The idea of taking time away from academics to build this feeling of "we-ness" is often easier for elementary teachers than for middle and high school teachers to embrace. Although teachers at all levels feel the pressure to move their students through mandated curricula, elementary teachers, perhaps because they have the same students for a good portion of the day, seem more able to incorporate community-building activities into their day. At the middle and high school levels, where teachers see a student for 40 to 50 minutes once a day, the pressure to begin content work immediately is difficult to resist. Yet doing so results in a substantial increase in disruptive behavior among students at all levels. What we found in our observations and interviews was that teachers who spent time getting to know students and having students get to know them and one another often had fewer problems in their classrooms. The better the job of laying this foundation and creating a sense of community, the better students' academic work will be later. Time spent at the beginning will indeed be made up later, when time does not need to be spent on resolving behavioral disturbances.

RULES AND PROCEDURES

Teachers with low-aggression classrooms teach rules, procedures, and consequences as explicitly as they teach content. Rules are guidelines governing appropriate and inappropriate student behaviors. Procedures are what students need to know in order to meet their own personal needs and to perform routine instructional and "housekeeping" activities. Successful teachers also spend time monitoring their students and applying appropriate consequences in a caring and consistent way. Teachers effective in this manner typically integrate their rules, procedures, and consequating efforts into a workable classroom routine. Time spent on such matters is not seen as taking time away from the curriculum. Instead, such teachers recognize that if one is spending a good portion of the day dealing with disruptions, material is not going to be covered anyway. Therefore, they see their first teaching task as minimizing disruptions, and they willingly spend as much time on this as necessary.

The teaching of rules and procedures begins on the first day of school. Ideally, teachers meet students at the classroom door and, in a friendly but firm manner, direct students to their seats—either assigned in elementary or random until assigned in middle and high school. This effort communicates the first procedure that the teacher expects to be followed—how to enter the classroom. It also establishes the teacher as the leader in the classroom. Often on the first day the teacher puts his or name and an outline of the activities for that day on the chalkboard. This sets the tone for the class and introduces another procedure—students should always check the board for the day's assignment upon entering.

The teacher then introduces himself or herself, calls roll, and spends a large block of time involving students in the creation of rules. Rules usually come first, with procedures being taught as they come up during the course of the first week. The best rules for making rules are:

- Keep them few in number (three to six).
- Negotiate them with the students.
- State them behaviorally and positively.
- Contract them with the students.
- Send them home to parents.
- Post them in the classroom.

In an elementary classroom, where the teacher has the students all day, this discussion of rules and procedures will probably happen on and off throughout the first few days of school, as the need arises. Elementary teachers often make the setting up of rules their first class-building exercise. They have clear in their minds what rules they need for their class to function successfully, but, rather than just stating them, they elicit the rules from the students. This gives the students a sense of ownership and promotes rule adherence. Rules are always stated in a positive, behavioral way ("Listen quietly while others are speaking" rather than "Don't interrupt other people"), and time is allowed for discussion of the rules, why they are important, and examples.

The next step for the elementary teacher is contracting the rules. Even very young children can understand the idea of making contracts. By signing a contract they are agreeing to follow the rules. It is also a good idea at this point to send a copy of the classroom rules home for parents to read and sign. The list of rules is sent home with a letter explaining that the rules were drawn up by the class as a whole, their child has signed a copy of the rules, and the teacher would like the parents to review the rules with their child and sign and return the letter to indicate that they have done so. Sending rules home in this manner paves the way for home-school collaboration, discussed in the next section.

The last step for establishing rules in the elementary classroom is posting them. Posting rules reminds students what the rules are. In addition, when a rule is broken, the teacher can point to the posted rule for its reaffirmation.

In a secondary classroom the teacher also introduces himself or herself, calls role, and spends a large block of time presenting rules. The rules are generally the same at the secondary level as at the elementary level. However, when the teacher sees between 130 to 150 students a day, negotiating rules with students can be difficult. In middle school, some teachers list the rules (again, stated positively and behaviorally) during each class and have class discussions, during which time students come up with rule examples. This class-building exercise may need to go on for more than the first day. Other teachers divide the class into groups and have each group come up with a set of rules. The teacher explains that once all the classes have done this he or she will then take all the ideas and integrate them into a final consensus set. The teacher then shows the classes how the rules they end up with are the direct result of what they generated. A discussion of the final rules, with concrete examples, is then held with each class.

Ninth graders also need to spend this kind of time on rules. In most school districts, they are part of the high school and are in a new building with a new administration and new rules. By tenth, eleventh, and twelfth grades this time might not have to be spent. Instead, rules can be briefly stated and examples given.

In both middle school and high school, rules should be contracted with the students. In the middle school and ninth grade, rules should be sent home in a letter to parents for signatures. In tenth, eleventh, and twelfth grades students should be given a copy of the rules. Rules should be posted at all levels except high school.

Because at this level many teachers may use one room, some teachers do and some do not post rules.

Classroom procedures are equally important in both elementary and secondary schools. In the average classroom, between 30 and 60 procedures are necessary to keep a room running smoothly. In the elementary classroom, students usually have one or two teachers whose procedures they must learn. Middle school and high school students may have as many as eight or nine teachers with different sets of procedures to learn. At both levels, it is well worth the time for teachers to think through, as carefully and fully as possible, how they want their classes to operate. The more thorough and complete teachers are in establishing a routine and the more consistently that routine is followed, the less chance for disruption in the classroom. In other words, no matter what method of delivering instruction you are using—direct instruction, learning centers, or cooperative learning—your classroom procedures need to be very structured and explicitly taught to students. You cannot assume that students know these things. They must be taught what *you* expect of them. Your procedures must cover everything that goes on in the room, including what to do when first entering, talking among students, obtaining help, sharpening pencils, leaving the room, returning to the room, using bathroom passes, interrupting, following fire and disaster procedures, working with classroom helpers, asking questions, disposing of trash, and any others appropriate for your classroom.

These procedures are taught as the need for them comes up in the classroom. As with rules, procedures need to be clearly stated, closely monitored, consistently followed, and consequated when not followed. We found that consistency—with procedural expectations being clearly defined for students and enforced every time, for everyone, no exceptions—to be a key factor in maintaining a low-aggression environment. Consistent application of rules and procedures provides clear expectations for student behavior, gives students the message that the teacher is aware of their behavior, and establishes that the teacher is in charge of the classroom. Yet such consistency is difficult to maintain over time. Teachers get tired, bored, or overworked, and sometimes it seems easier to "let it go just this once." In the long run, "just this once" can become more than once, and the message students receive is that the boundary between what is acceptable and unacceptable is no longer firm. Several of the teachers we interviewed reported that as soon as students sense that the expectations have been lowered even slightly, they start pushing to find where the boundary is, and the foundation for the safe, low-aggression space where learning can occur begins to erode. "Every time with every child" seems to be the motto of successful teachers.

As a related point, teachers who have been in a building for more than a couple of years and have established a reputation for being "strict" (that often means firm but fair in kid talk) have an easier time. Although such teachers get new students every year, their reputations precede them, and it does not take them nearly as long as a new teacher to establish the desired low-aggression climate.

HOME-SCHOOL COLLABORATION

Schools have always sought home-school contact, but many times contact has meant the school (the experts) telling the parents (the nonexperts) what to do. Traditionally, contact has taken the form of PTA meetings, room parenting, or parent-teacher conferences, in which the educators tell the parents about their child. Teachers who have low aggression levels in their classrooms often view parents differently. They recognize and appreciate parents as the child's first teachers, and they actively seek contact early and frequently, seeing this contact as an opportunity to collaborate in a supportive, mutually reinforcing way. In this way the parents, the teacher, and the child have the potential to become a problem-solving team. The opportunity for the child to be successful is thus greatly enhanced. Because children who succeed in school are much less likely to be disruptive, aggression in the classroom is diminished.

For elementary teachers, early contact often takes the form of an introductory letter to the home before school starts. The main purpose of the letter is to welcome the child and the parents to the teacher's class. The teacher introduces himself or herself, talks about some of the activities planned for the school year, and ends with an invitation to the parents and child to the first open house (which ideally is held early in the school year). An invitation to the parents to call the teacher at any time with questions or concerns (at a school telephone number) is included. The teacher also invites the parents to visit the classroom by setting up an appointment and tells them to expect an introductory phone call, just to get acquainted, within the first weeks of school. In this way the groundwork for a successful partnership with the home is laid.

This first phone call, made before there are any problems with the child, is very important. The tone should be friendly, with the teacher's saying something positive about the child and his or her academic potential. It is also very important at this initial stage to establish a collaborative atmosphere in which the parents feel they are valued members of a team whose purpose is to help the child be successful in school. Too often parents are seen as the enemy, and any contacts are made in such a way that the parents get the message that the teacher feels the problems with the youngster are the parents' fault. This immediately puts the parents on the defensive and causes an alliance to be drawn of parents-child versus teacher. Better, via the outreach of the teacher, that the alliance become a team effort of parents, teacher, and child. If a problem does develop that requires contact, it is much easier to deal with friendly parents than with hostile ones. The interaction then becomes a problem-solving process in which both parents and teacher try to come up with ways to modify the child's behavior. Having the support of the parents of a disruptive child may not solve the problem entirely, but it often helps a great deal.

At the middle and high school levels, it becomes impossible to make phone calls to 130 to 150 families. At these levels, teachers who maintain low-aggression classrooms often make early initial contact with parents via a letter home introducing themselves, giving a brief course description, articulating classroom rules and homework expectations, and extending an invitation to call the teacher at school about any concerns or problems. Then if a child is disruptive and a phone contact is necessary, an initial friendly contact has been established.

All phone calls should start with a positive statement about the child. Nothing puts parents on the defensive faster than to have a teacher start a conversation with "Your child is a real problem, and I won't stand for this behavior in my classroom." Once you have defensive parents, it is very difficult to gain their trust and help. They may argue with you and deny that their child causes problems, or they may "yes" you just to get you off the phone. In either case, when they get off the phone they may well turn to their child and agree with him or her that you are a jerk and it is not worth paying attention to you. Either way, your chance of parental help is gone. Remaining positive opens the door for parents and teachers to problem solve together.

Although some parents will at first be surprised and a little hesitant to participate in a problem-solving session if they have not been approached this way before, most will respond in a positive way once they realize that the teacher is sincerely asking for a collaborative relationship. Many parents do not know how to help their children be successful in school. Home-school collaboration can encourage this success.

Home-school collaboration needs to be more than just phone calls or letters home. It should include inviting the parents to be a part of the learning environment of the classroom. It is often difficult for teachers to manage a classroom alone, given the variety of needs that different children have. A parent volunteer who has been trained in the workings of a classroom can provide the additional support that teachers need. Research shows that the achievement of students in a school where there is a high degree of parental involvement, even if it is not by the children's own parents, is frequently greater than that of students in a school where there is virtually no involvement.

In an elementary classroom, a parent might be invited to work with an individual student on skill development or to help with a small group of children when the teacher is working with the rest of the class. Inviting a parent (or grandparent) to lend a hand with a special project or to actually teach a skill, trade, or hobby to the entire class could also be effective. In some elementary schools, programs for family math and parent and child literacy have been successful.

In middle and high schools, parents are not always welcomed by their own children due to peer pressure. The challenge for middle school and high school teachers and parents is to design programs that encourage participation in ways that will not embarrass their children. This might involve the parents' working in classes other than their own children's or working outside of the classroom with students who need extra help. In both of these instances, parent connectedness to the academic enterprise in general and the school in particular is heightened, thus increasing the chances of both parent attentiveness to the child's academic progress and parent receptivity to teacher initiatives, should the child engage in aggressive behaviors. Although it may be harder to achieve parent involvement at the secondary level, it is imperative that the attempt be made.

In these challenging times, when discipline is often difficult to maintain, home-school collaboration can serve two purposes. First, by creating a positive relationship with parents from the beginning, parents and teachers can work together as a problem-solving team if behavioral problems do occur. Again, it is much easier to work with supportive parents than hostile ones. Second, helping parents support and encourage their children's academic achievement creates a climate in which the child has a better chance of being academically successful—and the child who is more successful academically has higher self-esteem and is less disruptive in the classroom.

As teachers, we need to break down the long tradition of isolation from colleagues and from parents. Keeping in mind that both educators and parents are concerned about the well-being of children, we must take the initiative of working side by side in the educational process.

PHYSICAL CHARACTERISTICS OF THE CLASSROOM

What might a low-aggression classroom look like? First, its door is solidly constructed, not easily broken or broken through. The door contains a window enabling someone looking in to view most of the classroom and someone inside to survey the hallway. The door is attached to its frame by hydraulic dampers so that the harder one pushes, the slower the door closes. In addition, the door is key lockable, permitting the teacher to keep intruders out. The teacher's desk is also of solid construction and, as is true for all the desks and tables in the room, bolted to the floor so that it cannot be used to block anyone's movement, upturned as a blockade, or picked up and thrown in the midst of a fight. Furthermore, it is placed strategically in the room to maximize the teacher's ability to see the room, move about the room, and, if necessary, escape from the room. Student desks or tables are arranged with sufficient space between them to minimize potential crowding and inadvertent bumping. Instead, both the layout and grouping of student furniture eases movement by students as transitions take place, as well as teacher access to students. Any call-for-assistance devices in the room are also easily accessed by the teacher. The floor plan allows the teacher to move swiftly about the room or even exit for reasons of personal safety.

What else might characterize this hypothetical classroom? There are few, if any, hidden corners or closets. There are few, if any, objects lying around that might serve as weapons, such as staplers or scissors. All such materials are marked for identification and kept in a locked closet under teacher control. The storage area is located so the teacher is able to continue viewing the class at the same time materials are being retrieved. The room is well lit, its lights are key (not switch) controlled, and its windows are small and made of unbreakable material. The entire window area is covered with decorative grillwork. The interior of the room is painted at least in part in bright colors with a hard-surface paint. Little or no graffiti or other marks of vandalism exist in the room because whenever such defacement takes place it is swiftly recorded, removed, and repaired. Because of successful teacher efforts to help the students feel that the classroom is *their* room, such vandalism is infrequent. Instead, the room expresses the class's personal touch—a plant here, a cushioned area there, a few fresh and interesting wall displays of student work, and similar evidence that "This is our place."

Although these accommodations will help minimize aggression, some of them plainly have a negative side. Bolting classroom furniture to the floor to prevent its being used as a weapon or blockade will also prevent its imaginative regrouping for classroom community building and other positive purposes. Grillwork over classroom windows will diminish the frequency of the single most common form of school vandalism—broken windows; it will also just as certainly increase the sense of "prisonization" that has befallen many of our schools. For these reasons, we urge that physical alterations in the classroom be made cautiously. Changes should reflect the nature and severity of the aggression level in your class, your school, and your community.

We have considered, in this chapter, what appear to be the characteristics of a classroom setting in which low levels of student aggression prevail. These characteristics include in-depth understanding of one's students; comprehensive preplanning of classroom activities; heavy reliance on efficient, student-oriented instructional behaviors; major efforts to create a sense of community; effective development and implementation of classroom rules and procedures; a serious and continuing commitment to creatively facilitate home-school collaboration; and an array of physical alterations and accommodations in the classroom. That these features of the low-aggression classroom are not easy to accomplish is clear, but equally clear is that energetic efforts toward their implementation can yield substantial rewards in terms of better classroom management, student achievement, and quality of the classroom experience for both students and teachers.

NOTES

1. See, for example, J. Kounin, *Discipline and group management in classrooms* (New York: Holt, Rinehart and Winston, 1970).

2. Examples of such games and simulations appear in J. Gibbs, *Tribes* (Santa Rosa, CA: Center Source Publications, 1987) and A. P. Goldstein, *The Prepare Curriculum: Teaching prosocial competencies*. (Champaign, IL: Research Press, 1988), as well as in other sources.

Aggressive Incidents
and Their Lessons

As noted in the introduction, this book is for teachers and by teachers. This focus is especially reflected in the present chapter. The nature and management of student aggression may be informed by relevant educational and psychological theory, by both quantitative and qualitative research, by school administrators and security personnel, by parents and students, and by other means. Here, however, we rely on the experiences and insights of those designated by society to be the frontline observers, intervenors, and often targets of aggressive behavior—classroom teachers.

Our goal was to obtain from teachers a broad, national sample of descriptions of student aggression at varying levels of severity and how these incidents were dealt with. By a variety of means—interviews, snowball sampling, direct solicitation through district offices or school administrators, and distribution in eight geographically dispersed states of a "Send Us Your Fights" flyer—we obtained 1,000 incident reports. Experienced and novice male and female teachers in urban, suburban, and rural schools at the elementary, middle, and senior high school levels are fully represented. To process this rich incident pool and draw from it aggression management lessons, each of us independently studied the 1,000 reports, considered them at length, and evaluated their likely value. Our collective judgments and recommendations form the basis for the lessons derived in this chapter.

The incidents are grouped into the 15 broad topical categories listed in Table 1. We have attempted to present the first 13 categories in ascending order of severity. Generally, horseplay, rules violation, disruptiveness, refusal, and cursing are low-level expressions of aggression. Bullying, sexual harassment, physical threats, and vandalism are midlevel expressions. Out-of-control behavior, fights, attacks on teachers, and group aggression are high-level forms.

Send Us Your Fights!

We are a small group of semibattered, but not defeated, classroom teachers (plus one School of Education professor), trying to put together a really practical and useful guidebook for fellow teachers on how to handle student aggression. We know that aggression is an immense problem in more and more American schools and that many, many teachers are faced almost daily with the challenge of resolving fights, preventing escalation, minimizing violence and vandalism. We also know that many of the best solutions to such problems come from practicing teachers themselves, out on the frontline. We want to help teachers learn from each other by putting together a casebook of student aggression incidents and how they were handled. So, please send us your fights!

Specifically, we seek and would welcome brief descriptions (a page or two) of student-student, student-teacher, or other in-school aggressive incidents. All that your description need include are details on what happened and how the situation was handled. We will put these incidents together and try to suggest the lessons that we can learn and use from them.

If you can participate in this effort, please feel free to send us one or more descriptions of incidents at any grade level, at any aggression level (mild, moderate, severe), and at any level of success, i.e., we want incidents with a good aggression-reducing outcome, but also those that didn't work out so well. We can learn from both. Your contributions to this effort will be greatly appreciated.

TABLE 1

Incident Categories

1. Horseplay

2. Rules Violation

3. Disruptiveness

4. Refusal

5. Cursing

6. Bullying

7. Sexual Harassment

8. Physical Threats

9. Vandalism

10. Out-of-Control Behavior

11. Fights

12. Attacks on Teachers

13. Group Aggression

14. Exemplars

15. Special Topics

Grouping the incidents into categories better helps us extrapolate lessons from them; however, it is important to note that overlap exists among the categories and that any act of aggression can escalate quickly into a serious situation. In fact, it is only possible to judge the level of severity of an aggressive incident in the specific context in which it occurs. What we can say, however, is that poor management of aggression at the lower levels facilitates its high-level expression. Conversely, the teacher skilled at maintaining compliance or thwarting student disruptiveness is, we believe, considerably less likely to be faced subsequently with vandalistic, out-of-control, or armed students. "Catch it low, prevent it high" is a productive intervention strategy.

The last two categories, exemplars and special topics, include, respectively, incidents reflecting especially competent teacher management and incidents reflecting important dimensions of aggression management not covered in other categories.

Finally, in this chapter we seek to let teachers speak to teachers. The incidents reported share much from the frontlines of America's classrooms that is instructive for the management of student aggression. Along with courage and creativity, the incidents illustrate victories and defeats, competence and incompetence, wisdom and, in some instances, its absence. Although each aggressive incident at school is unique, we hope the lessons shared here will prove useful in the ever-more-difficult and demanding task of teaching in the contemporary classroom.

Horseplay

The typical textbook definition of aggression is intentional physical or psychological injury to another person. Horseplay— expressed in such behaviors as poking, pushing, teasing, "dissing," "play-fighting," and similar actions—may well begin as, and be intended as, fun. However, as the incidents in this section clearly demonstrate, such fun frequently escalates.

(1) I was alone in the room with the students, and they started horsing around, and then the horseplay became more of a fight. I had one student becoming very aggressive with my other student, who is not aggressive himself and not able really to defend himself. So [the first student] started picking [the second] up and was kind of tossing him around the room, on the floor and on the desks, so I went over and I managed to get them separated the first time. . . . No sooner did I get them separated and they were fighting again. At that point I went over to try and start to separate them again, and another student blocked my way so I couldn't get over to them. And then what I had was two students fighting and the one being much stronger and very aggressive and acting out anyway, and was really hurting the one student. . . . I really couldn't work my way through. . . . At that point the student who was hurting the other student . . . slammed him down on the ground, and he hurt his head. . . . The one blocking me . . . moved out of the way, and the other student was briefly unconscious. At that time I had to ring the buzzer to get the nurse in to have help come down in case anything else broke out. And the nurse came, and then the principal came right down. . . . It would have been nice if there had been reinforcement closer and another person in the room or something to get it broken up quicker. But because I'm back in the school kind of off by myself, it's really hard for anybody to hear anything going on.

The lesson is, if you need assistance to stop horseplay or the fight that may grow out of it, call for that help early in the incident and not, as happened here, after it has escalated.

As the next incident illustrates, if not swiftly and effectively interrupted, horseplay with staff also may grow into more serious levels of student aggression. The line between legitimate play and play with substantial potential for trouble should be drawn conservatively.

> (2) On August 7, a student and a staff member were playing around with each other (throwing water on each other). This alleged incident took place at [the state park] as the students and staff were to be boarding the bus to return to N. School.
>
> Allegedly, the student put a substance in the water that he threw, and the staff member responded by putting catsup on the student. The student became angry and picked up an iron garbage can, throwing it at the staff member, missing him but hitting a black 1991 Grand Prix automobile, causing extensive damage to the left fender of the vehicle. The owner of the vehicle was notified and a report was taken by the park patrol.

Besides actively participating in horseplay, teachers may contribute to escalation of an incident by responding in kind to a challenging youth, as Incident 3 shows.

> (3) As I entered the room I noted the boy in question was lifting another boy off the floor by the collar. The other child was sort of laughing, attempting not to antagonize the more aggressive boy. I simply asked K. to take his hands off M.
>
> K. ignored me and continued to lift up M., who was laughing less by the moment. I gave the same verbal direction again, with no response. At this point no one was laughing. I walked over to the two boys and pried K.'s fingers off M., using some backwards leverage to remove his fingers.
>
> K. then lost it and started telling me he was going to punch me in the face. I guess this struck me as ludicrous, (I am 5' 11" and this boy is about 5' 2", and I probably outweighed him by at least 50 pounds). . . . Forgetting my better judgment

I stepped toward him and said, "Try it and see what the consequences are."

K. backed off and started making fun of my clothes and my hair. Once again I probably did not use good judgment as I responded, "What makes you think I even care how you think I look?" . . . At this point another teacher whipped in and whisked him off to the principal's office for threatening a teacher.

At times horseplay evolves into an attack on a teacher, even when the teacher does intervene swiftly and properly to stop the behavior, as done in Incident 4. Rapid intervention by school security personnel was effective in this instance. Note the common phenomenon of the same events being described rather differently by the main participants—the teaching assistant (victim), teacher (witness), and student (perpetrator).

(4A—Teaching assistant) On Thursday, November 29, at approximately 1:47 P.M., I was walking [K.] from gym. . . . On the way, L. was trying to box with him. I asked [L.] to stop. I then intervened—he continued. Then when I got to the staircase, on the right side of the main office, L. punched me in my left arm very forcefully. I immediately walked into the office to get a referral form. Mrs. P. witnessed L. punching me in the arm. On the way back to class, L. was still hanging out in the halls. He then said, "Oh, you're writing a referral on me. I don't care— I'll punch you in your face." He began to box around with his fists up in the air. It was then when Officer M. intervened.

(4B—Teacher) At 1:35 P.M., Friday, November 30, I was returning from the gym with my students. It was class passing time for the secondary students. I was walking behind Ms. G. (she was escorting her class from the gym also). L. was approaching from the opposite direction. As he passed Ms. G., he punched her very hard in the upper left arm. I heard the smack of the impact even though there was noise of students passing between classes.

(4C—Student) Mrs. Q., Ms. G., S., and I was playing in the gym. So we was playing and stuff. On the way out the gym Mrs. Q. punch me in the arm and grab my neck. It hurted a little bit, but I never thought nothing of it because we was playing. So we walked a little further, and we was still playing, and I hit Ms. G. in the arm. She took it seriously, but I thought we was still playing. She didn't give me time to apologize. She just wrote me a referral.

In contrast to the use of school security, in Incident 5 the effective intervention after escalated horseplay was undertaken by the school's administrator, who properly issued a suspension and involved the youth's parents in both the intervention and return to school.

(5) All right, lunch started off with a little bit of food throwing, escalating, for some reason. At least one of the students really took it very seriously and soon just lost control. He wanted to throw chairs, and within a matter of . . . a minute or so, he was . . . out of control. . . . He was running down the length of the cafeteria, and the counselor tackled his legs, and I held his arms. . . . I said . . . "I won't let go until you talk and say all right I'm going to walk." By the time we actually got in the office—it's quite a ways down there—down this long hall, he had cooled down, and then at that point I really didn't have anything to do with it— the principals took over. . . . He couldn't come back to school until a parent came up to reinstate him, and I think he had 3 days before he could do that.

Especially with elementary students, firm and consistent reiteration by the teacher of previously announced and agreed upon classroom rules and penalties for their violation will prove to be an effective way of stopping horseplay. Incident 6 demonstrates this approach.

(6) Class is doing a project involving salt maps. As they work, noise level rises and some students begin to play with dough, throwing it at each other and up in the air instead of putting it on cardboard for maps. Teacher holds up hand till it starts to get quiet and says, "It has to be quieter in here, and the playing has to stop." Class continues to talk loud and play with dough. Teacher again raises hand and as it begins to quiet down she says, "How many

of you want to continue working on this today?" (All but two raise their hands.) "How many of you are willing to talk in quiet voices and stop playing in order to work on this today?" (Again, all but two raise their hands.) "Good, because if it continues to be noisy and the playing doesn't stop and people don't get to work, then we will stop for today." Groups settle down and start working. Obviously, this teacher has said this before and stopped an activity that got out of hand because [students] clearly believe her when she says settle down or we will stop.

When horseplay escalates to a student fight, as Incident 7 shows, a stronger teacher-administrator response is appropriate.

(7) K. and G. had both been asked repeatedly to stop fooling around (they seemed to be friends), talking, picking at each other, etc. and sit down to research papers. . . . I thought they had done just that—K. was sitting down, and G. was at the table. All at once K. jumped out of her seat and started waling on G. . . . I put my arms out to separate them—the table fell over, stuff flew off my desk. . . . Finally we moved in front of the desk—I asked them to stop, count, cool-off, sit down, and so on. . . . He finally sat—then she did. K. continued to shout and jump up, but everything was "cooled" as Mr. M. entered to remove students from room.

The students in this escalation of horseplay were likely too pumped up and out of control for simple reiteration of classroom rules to be adequate for quieting the scene. Instead, the teacher separated the youths without interposing herself physically, then calmly and repeatedly stated "stop, count, cool-off, sit down" instructions as the help, called for in a timely manner, arrived.

Rules Violation

Both teacher experience and research have underscored the valuable contribution of classroom rules, properly developed and enforced, toward minimizing student aggression. As noted in chapter 1, such rules should be few in number, negotiated with students, stated behaviorally and positively, contracted with students, sent home to parents, and posted in the classroom. Employment of these "rules for rules" will enhance student motivation to comply with rule enactment. If a rule feels (and perhaps is) arbitrary, authoritarian, or irrelevant to the educational, safety, or social-interactional purpose of schooling, student adherence will diminish, rule violation will increase, and both student-student and student-teacher strife will be more likely to occur. Perhaps one of the best current examples of a rule whose difficulty of enforcement is causing aggression is the injunction against wearing hats. Like other rules, the rule against wearing hats should be employed depending on the circumstances and climate of one's own school.

In each of the following incidents, precipitous enforcement of a "hat rule" seems to have more to do with exercising control than instilling courtesy. The result is a rapid escalation of student aggression. One might title these three incidents "The Hat Tug of War," "Snatch Off Head," and "Keep in the Office Till June."

> (8) I saw [K.] standing in the hall with his hat on. I had previously asked student to remove it twice. K. began wrestling in the hall with another student. I asked them to stop wrestling. K.'s hat fell off. I picked up the hat and told K. to pick up his hat from the main office at the end of the day. Student became aggressive and grabbed his hat. I continued to hang on to it. I asked K. to go to the office. He started to swear and said, "I'm sick of people taking my shit." Student pushed me and continued to swear. I asked student to stop—did not. E. G. and K. C. came down the hallway at this time and helped escort K. into the office.

(9A—Teacher) L. was told several times by several different staff members to take off his hat. He ignored all requests. He would touch his hat each time but not take it off (as if he was taunting us). He began to walk into the office (without permission). I told him that if he didn't take his hat off, I would. He didn't, and I did. He followed me out of the office and down the hall, leaning on me all the way. I told him to back off me. He did not. He then said, "Give me my fucking hat." He then pushed me. I began to escort him to the office. He started to wrestle with me by grabbing my legs and pulling me up. We both fell to the floor. He did not release from me until he was pulled away from me. After he was pulled away from me, he slapped me across the face.

(9B—Student) I was walking to the office, and Mr. N. had hit me on the head and snatched my hat off my head. He had told me one time before to take off my hat, so he took it off me in a mean way. So I tried to get my hat back, and he pushed me, and I pushed him back. Then he tried to put me on the ground, then we both got on the ground, then we both got on the ground wrestling. It wouldn't of never started if he wouldn't of pushed me and almost made me slip on the wet floor.

(10) On Friday at dismissal, C. became very upset because I would not return a hat he had been wearing during school. (C. had been repeatedly informed of the policy on hat wearing but refused to comply. In such situations, I keep the hat until June or until a caretaker picks the item up.) C. refused to leave on his bus and attempted to get his hat back by searching through my desk drawers. During this search, C. pushed me around, grabbed me by the shoulder, and threatened to punch me if I did not return his hat. I called the office to request assistance. [Mrs. X.] arrived several minutes later. She reminded C. of the policy on hats in school and cautioned him to take his bus home. C. did not comply; he was combative, refused to leave, and continued his threatening tone with Mrs. X. During this time C. was creating a continuous disruption by buzzing the office, etc. An attempt was made to reach his mother to pick him up. When it appeared as though that was unsuccessful, the police were called to escort C. home. Just after their arrival, C.'s brother showed up to take him home.

In this era of student preoccupation with "respect," we urge that whenever possible confrontations about hat wearing and other issues be carried out nonpublicly (i.e., by the teacher's taking the student aside to reiterate the rule without an audience or escorting the student to the office). Student adherence to *any* rule the school seriously wishes to enforce will best be accomplished if the consequences meted out are put into effect swiftly, consistently, and in a businesslike manner, with minimal rancor. This is true whether the consequence is a brief loss of privilege or stay in time-out or, for more serious infractions, a call to parents or police, suspension, or expulsion. A rule violation not consequated at all is, in all probability, likely to result in the behavior's reoccurrence. Such was the case in Incident 11.

> (11) One of the district's rules that is often repeated by the administration is that students cannot share food because of the hepatitis scare. Two girls were walking down the hall sharing a cold hamburger. They were also late for class. I walked toward them and asked them to stop sharing the food and put it away. One responded with "This ain't none of your business!" The other retorted, "You can't tell us what to do!" I repeated my original request that they put the food away and get to class. One of the girls grabbed a piece of the burger as she began to walk fast to class. To be spiteful, the other girl took her time walking to class, turning around to see if I was still watching her.

An appropriate consequence for a rule violation or more serious transgression is one that is in fact experienced negatively by the youth. In Incident 12, a different, more boring time-out location or provision of an alternative consequence (e.g., loss of free-play time or other privilege) might have been appropriate.

> (12) Teacher has rules posted around room as mind maps. Students enter and are asked to complete work on board. Those who don't start immediately are approached by the teacher and asked to begin. Teacher goes over questions from board, and one girl gets out of her seat and walks to another girl to talk. Teacher asks girl to return to seat, and she replies, "Wait a minute." Teacher writes student's name on board and announces that one more time will result in time-out. Girl replies, "So what?"

The student's rule violation behavior may be followed by an appropriate consequence, but not swiftly enough. In Incident 13, the student's initial verbal expressions of aggression are met by reiteration of the rule. It is only late in the escalation sequence, when the student lunges at the teacher, that the student is escorted to the office and given an in-school suspension.

(13) Approximately 100 students were selected to attend a field trip in November. Three of the four buses arrived to school, and the students and chaperons boarded, then waited for the fourth bus. Myself, two other teachers, our teacher on special assignment, and a group of students waited outside the buses for ours to arrive. Everyone was very patient and polite.

For some reason there exists a rule that bus windows are not supposed to be open. This rule has been in effect since September. While standing outside the third bus, I noticed the back seat window was open. I asked the girl inside to close the window. She snapped back, "Who the hell is she to tell me what to do?" I then asked her more firmly to close the window. She responded that she did not have to. The teacher on special assignment was standing outside the second bus. I told her about the lack of cooperation I was receiving from a student unfamiliar to me. I described the girl to this woman, and she knew exactly who I was talking about.

The teacher on special assignment called the girl off the bus and she calmly spoke with her one-to-one. I went back to my group and mingled with the students and other teachers. Suddenly, the girl came lunging towards me, pointing her finger at me, screaming, "I hate you! I hate you!" over and over again. The teacher on special assignment had to take her by the arm and escort her in the building. The whole time she continued screaming, "I hate you! You're an old, white bitch!" This behavior continued until they reached the office. . . .

The student was put in in-school suspension [ISS] for the remainder of the day. While in ISS, she constantly complained about the white bitch . . . who put her in suspension. The

29

ISS teacher repeatedly told her to be quiet and eventually sent her back to the office, where they called home.

The teacher in Incident 14 does consequate swiftly but unfortunately also quickly gets into a shouting match and power struggle with the student, a struggle in which there are no ultimate winners. Teaching is often a stressful and frustrating profession. Nevertheless, the likelihood of further rule violation diminishes if one can avoid or minimize heated battles and with relative calmness: (a) state the rule, (b) state the consequences, and (c) consistently carry out the consequences.

> (14) Seventh-grade classroom. No rules posted. Beginning of class. . . . Students enter room and take seats. . . . Teacher enters. After door is closed, a young man enters. Teacher tells student that he has detention since he was late: "You know the rule—late to class equals detention." Child responds that he "ain't staying." Teacher reprimands and asks him to sit in seat. He continues to sputter about not staying. She continues to reprimand about how he broke the rule and he has to suffer the consequences. He then yells at her and again repeats that he's not staying, adding that "I hate this class, and I hate you, too." Teacher then screams at kid to leave—she will send a referral. After kid leaves, she reprimands rest of class (who had been quiet) and proceeds to write out referral.

In the next two incidents, common objects typically found in the classroom are employed as weapons by students engaged in heated arguments with their teachers about rule violations. In Incident 15, the weapon (a pen) fortunately is not used for the threatened assault, though the teacher makes the sometimes difficult-to-avoid mistake of touching the student. When thrown, a stapler becomes a weapon in Incident 16. Cases like these prompt us, reluctantly but of necessity, to urge teachers to think and act defensively in their classrooms. Perhaps one further classroom rule is worth considering, an "environmental prevention" rule by which teacher desks and other classroom surfaces have only paper on them, with all heavy or sharp objects being kept in a locked drawer or closet.

> (15) T. was talking to M. (seated in front of her) during taking a test and got loud, rude, and upset when I took 20 points

off her test for this situation. Both girls had a warning prior not to talk (and they've known all year about test-taking procedures).

When the bell rang 10 minutes later, T. came up to my desk, demanded that I take her out of my class, and said she hated me and this "fucking class." As we walked to the door, T. was still swearing and slammed her books on the floor outside the door. She turned and started approaching me, pushing toward me (body was pushing me) and stuck her pen in my face, saying she should "knock my fucking face off." I put my hand on her arm, and she pushed it off, saying she didn't like me touching her. I replied she'd better leave . . . and go to the office or wherever, but just go! . . .

After about 2 minutes of this swearing and pushing, T. picked up her books and stormed off. My entire first-period class saw this mess as they tried to leave class.

(16) B. was writing in a library book with a black permanent magic marker. I asked her to stop because the noise was a high-pitched, squeaky sound, and the smell was offensive to everyone in the room. I also reminded her that we do not write in library books. She refused to stop. I asked her again, and she continued to write and disrupt the class. I told her that I would have to take the book and the marker away if she continued on. B. ignored me and the request made by many students in the class. I then removed the book and marker from B. She became very indignant, disruptive, and abusive. She came up to me and said, "Give me my book." I told her that I would give it to Mrs. D., and she could take care of it. B. continued to say, "Give me my book" over and over again. She then stated that if I did not give her the book she would throw something at me. I asked her to please sit down. She then walked over to Mrs. D.'s desk, picked up an object, and threw it at my head. I caught it in my left hand. My hand was and is still stinging—it is also bruised from the force she used to throw the heavy metal stapler. . . . I immediately called the office for assistance. Mr. S. came to the room and removed her.

This section's final three incidents each took place in lower elementary classrooms. As a group, especially as they contrast with

Incidents 8 through 16, they highlight the lesser (but far from absent) threat of violent repercussions in the behavior management of younger children. Each of these incidents also teaches us a further lesson relevant to our theme: Incident 17 illustrates the problems that may follow when a rule ("Stay in control of your body") is too abstract, in this case for a second-grade class. The more behaviorally concrete the rule, the more easily it is understood and the more readily it can be followed. Incident 18 exemplifies the value of combining the presentation of a rule with an explanation of its purpose. The less arbitrary and the more meaningful and relevant a rule is to students, the more likely it will be followed. Such adherence to rules will be even more likely, we believe, if teachers also employ along with rule restatement a procedure that may be the best way to prevent student aggression from emerging in the first place as well as to decrease the likelihood of its reemergence after an aggressive event. We speak here of "catch them being good"— providing praise, rewards, or recognition for nonaggressive, positive behaviors to either classmates of the rule violator (i.e., vicarious reinforcement) or to the rule violator himself or herself after subsequent rule compliance. Incident 19 illustrates how one teacher deals with a student's misbehavior by using this approach. We will provide further illustration of the value of "catch them being good" in later examinations of more serious forms of student aggression.

(17) Rules posted and reviewed at beginning of day. "Stay in control of your body" was explained. Two groups are on the floor, one at reading semicircle table. One child, a girl, was asked to keep her body under control as she kept inching forward (closer to another child) on the floor. At one time . . . the teacher asked her to get up and move three steps backwards.

(18) Teacher is at board reviewing steps of a project which has been started but not completed. Boys at one table are reading magazines while she is speaking. She goes over to them, still talking to rest of class, doesn't say anything, gathers up magazines, removes them from table, and puts them on a side table away from rest of class, never interrupting her whole class instruction. As she continues, talking erupts from another table in the class. She stops, raises her hand until talking subsides, and then says, "There's a group over

here that's talking while I am talking. That's a problem because if you're not listening now, then when it's time to work you'll be confused and won't know what to do." She then continues to give directions.

(19) Teacher doing group work with students in circle. Teacher in chair, students in circle on floor in front of teacher. Teacher showing students their names for them to identify. One student yells out name. Teacher calmly restates rules of exercise (everyone looks at name, but only student whose name it is can say the name out loud). Goes on with lesson. Holds up another name. Everyone is quiet and just student whose name is being shown calls out his/her name. Teacher says, "I like the way you all were quiet and let _____ have a chance to say their name. And _____, I like the way you called out your name when you saw it."

Disruptiveness

We have already stressed the fact that swift, consistent, and effective consequating of lower level student aggression is a strategy likely to minimize the escalation of such behavior to more serious and dangerous levels. The forms such escalation may take are well illustrated in this section's first three incidents, in which aggression—unconsequated or consequated inadequately—turns into disruptiveness by several students (Incident 20), an attack on another student (Incident 21), and an attack on a teacher (Incident 22).

> (20) The student became angry with the teacher because she returned a paper with a low grade on it. And he started going off, saying that she couldn't teach and when is she going to leave and so forth, and it got other kids riled, and they started complaining. And the teacher tried to calm [the student] down by saying that he could do make-up work and so forth, but the kids were complaining, and she had a hard time getting the kids settled.

> (21) This incident occurred with a freshman boy in an urban high school: The student had been mildly disruptive for several days and had to be excluded from class. For example, when he came in he would run around the room and jump up and down. Another day when class had started, he echoed back everything that I said. Another day he came in and hung paper clips from his nose and generally disrupted the class and had to be excluded across the hall. On this particular day, the student came in and ran around the room and went up and punched a young girl in the stomach. I called him out of class and brought him down to the office. When he was down in the office, he had time-out and was not allowed back in the room. He was assigned in-school suspension for the next day. During the next period I saw the student in the lunchline. The student said to me, "If you think I

gave you trouble before, you're really going to see trouble now. What you've already seen isn't anything. You're really going to have trouble come Tuesday when I'm back." I reported this to the principal, and this resulted in an informal hearing with the student.

(22) K. was told to remain inside the classroom to finish his work because he was disruptive and did not complete the assignment. He was to complete his work during the class recess period.

After the teacher took the class to the play group, she noticed that K. was outside playing, so she called him over and told him to return to the classroom (another teacher was on inside duty) to complete his work. K. said, "No, I'm not." The teacher took him by the hand and attempted to lead him toward the building. K. kicked the teacher on her leg, and as they were going up the steps, he pulled her down on the steps.

She was very sore, and her leg had a blue spot where she was kicked. K. was made to apologize, and he was placed in in-school suspension for a day.

Incident 20, involving disruptive complaining over a grade, might have been prevented or minimized had the teacher at the beginning of the year provided students and their parents with a clear, written statement of grading procedures. The teacher in Incident 21, in which the disruptive student punched another student, intervened in a variety of ways—exclusion from class, time-out, in-school suspension, referral for an administrative hearing. This energetic sequence of interventions did not appear to work. We wonder if greater success would have occurred if, following the first instance of disruptiveness, the youth's parents had been called for a conference. We will have more to say about parental involvement later. Here, we wish to offer the thought that it may have been the important missing piece. Finally, in Incident 22, the student severely kicked a teacher, for which the consequence was making him apologize and serve a day of in-school suspension. We feel strongly that a physical attack on another individual (student, teacher, administrator) is an assault and should be consequated as such. Perhaps in that small but growing number of district, city, and state school jurisdictions seeking to institute "zero-tolerance" consequating, cursing, disruptiveness, or bullying may warrant an apology and a day of in-school suspension. An assault is serious business, one often causing serious injury. More punitive consequences seem appropriate.

The provision of consequences to reduce student aggression or behaviors likely to lead to aggression must occur as soon as possible after the behavior one wishes to change. The teachers in the next three incidents do provide consequences—but much too slowly. One waits until the youth's fifth disruption (Incident 23), a second waits until the fourth day of disruptiveness (Incident 24), and a third arranges a parent conference at the end of May for disruptive behaviors appearing as early as the previous October (Incident 25). In each instance, the teacher's tolerance of unconsequated disruptiveness before finally acting rewards the youngster for disruptiveness, making it likely that the behavior will not change. In each of the three incidents delay perpetuates the disruptive behaviors the teachers sought to stop.

(23) W. was talking/laughing loudly during the class. He ignored me when I asked him to be quiet. I discussed class rules for the first 25 minutes of class. I asked him to be quiet and waited for him at least five times during the class period. I told him if he spoke again he'd be sent out—which happened. He then played in the hall—distracting students. I then sent him to the office. He left office without permission of teacher.

Administrative response: Two days out-of-school suspension.

(24) S. has been very disruptive during class—yelling out, refusing to do work, writing and drawing when she should be listening. This has been happening for 4 days now. There is no phone, but I have spoken with her sister.

Administrative response: Send note home by older sister.

(25) Constant disruptive behavior outside classroom. [The student] refused to answer or listen to me. He was warned yesterday and Thursday several times. He would not even look at me when I spoke to him.

Administrative response: In-school behavioral intervention program, parent conference. Parent must accompany D. back to school.

The teacher in Incident 26 takes a different intervention route, a favorite in America's schools—the use of reprimands. Observation in classrooms has shown that, beginning with second grade, the typical teacher in the United States issues one reprimand every 2 minutes![1] If one were to sit in the back of the average classroom and record all teacher comments, once every 2 minutes the entry would be "Stop that," "Don't go there," "Put that down," or a similar admonition. Although research on the effectiveness of reprimands for altering aggressive and other off-task behaviors is mixed, we remain skeptical about their usefulness. Aggression is a very stable behavior. The chronically aggressive school-age youth was almost invariably chronically aggressive as a preschool child and, as such, has been the recipient of hundreds of parental reprimands. Yet his or her aggressive behavior continues and often flourishes. Yes, we are skeptical about the effectiveness of reprimands. Incident 26 supports our skepticism.

> (26) The male student had been talking through the first part of a lesson and had been asked a few times to stop talking, and he didn't. . . . The more the teacher asked, the more the student refused. The teacher said, "I'm taking time away from 28 other students to deal with you. I want my classroom back. I want to start my lesson again." The student said, "Well, I'm not holding up the lesson. . . . You know you don't talk to anyone else. You just are telling me to be quiet and there's other people that are talking." [The teacher replied,] "I specifically asked you to be quiet, and that's why, that's what is taking up the time now." What ended up happening was the student was asked to leave the classroom. . . . He got an in-school suspension, and that was the end of the incident.

In Incident 23, the student was "talking/laughing loudly during class." In Incident 24, the student was "very disruptive during class—yelling out." Similarly intrusive behaviors are implied in Incident 25. In all three instances, it was impossible for the teacher to ignore the disruptive behaviors in the hope that inattention would result in their cessation. However, such use of extinction is possible when the disruptiveness is of a lower level and can be ignored without jeopardizing the teacher's ability to conduct class. The student in Incident 27 was playing with a piece of paper, and we wonder whether the teacher may have erred in "taking on" this behavior. As is true for many other forms of classroom acting out, disruptiveness is often undertaken to gain the reward of teacher and/or peer attention. Receiving the attention perpetuates the behavior. Withholding the attention may reduce or eliminate it. In Incident 27, the disruptiveness escalated to a serious physical attack on the teacher.

> (27) I took a piece of paper away from W. that she was repeatedly playing with. After I took the paper away, a couple scraps remained on her desk. She started putting them on her eyes, playing around, and laughing. I attempted to get them from her. She kept trying to hide them in her hand and in her overalls. A classmate sitting next to her tried to get them to help me. She hit him two times. When I called the office for help she gave me "the middle finger."
>
> When help came, she did not go willingly, and had to be escorted out of the room. She spent the next hour in the office. . . .
>
> As we lined up to go home, I noticed W. had something in her mouth. I asked her what. . . . She started running away. I grabbed her hand and tried looking in her mouth to see what it was and told her to open it—but she didn't. W. began to kick me and hit me. I continued holding her. She pinched me. . . . She also started biting me. . . .
>
> A teacher came to escort her to the office. She started walking with him—then resisted, and he picked her up and carried her to the office. In the office she threw pieces of paper at me. I walked away.

An alternative to extinction as a means of denying a youth the reward of attention for disruptive or other inappropriate behavior is time-out. In exclusion time-out, the youth is removed to a quiet place away from the opportunity to receive the admonishing attention of teachers and the approving attention of peers. Time-out should be time-out from not only attentional reward but other reinforcement, too. To be placed in a room with books, games, TV, peers, a window, and so on countervails the time-out-from-reward purpose of the procedure.

Mistakes in implementing time-out are common. One error is to place the youth in a dark, scary, confined place like a closet.

Removal from reward is being sought, not dungeon-like punishment. A second error is in being overly punitive by leaving the youth in time-out for very long periods, even hours. Time-out should generally end when the youth calms down, typically a period of 5 to 10 minutes.

Other time-out management errors are common. Some teachers enact time-out by sending the youth out of the classroom into the hall. Such was the case in Incident 23, already presented, as well as in the following incident. What might be more appropriately termed "hall detention" may—or, as we suspect, may not—serve a useful purpose. The opportunities provided to the youth by such placement to see and chat with passersby, enjoy perusing posted items on the corridor walls, and even roam about certainly do not conform to the goal of a proper time-out arrangement to reduce reinforcement.

(28) The next academic period [after lunch] was silent reading. Each student was given the opportunity to choose a book . . . to read. S. chose his book and immediately got out of his seat without permission to visit with another classmate. I asked him if he was following through with Rule 2 on the blackboard, which states, "Get permission by raising your hand to get out of seat." I received no answer from him. He just looked at me and smacked his lips together very loudly. He began to walk toward his seat but stopped off at the desk of another classmate to talk. I asked S. again if he was following class Rule 2. This time he stamped his left foot and walked very slowly to his desk. He sat down and started reading but began to make sounds which disrupted the class and me. I asked S. if he could please refrain from making those sounds. I reminded him that everyone was busy reading and that this is silent reading time. He began to hum out loud. Immediately, I asked if he needed some release time, out of the classroom to just calm down and think about how he can be just a little more cooperative with me and the class. He didn't respond. He started humming again. This time I asked S. to please leave the class for 10 minutes. . . . I opened the classroom door, and S. went out.

A final, and major, error in the use of time-out to reduce disruptiveness or other negative behaviors is to fail to carry it out in such a way that less (not more!) attention is provided to the youth.

Some teachers inappropriately supply this generous reward by the manner in which they bring the youth to or from the time-out location. The teacher in Incident 29 does so by joining the youth in the time-out location in order to discuss the disruptive event. Here, discussion may well have been an appropriate and useful problem-solving procedure, though not an appropriate time-out procedure.

(29) At approximately 11:00 A.M., while in gym class, D. was participating in a bat-and-ball game. I was reading, not really paying attention to the game. L. was pitching, and D. wasn't pleased with the job she was doing. Mr. I. wouldn't replace L., so D. got irritated and threw the ball across the gym. He was asked to sit out for 5 minutes by Mr. I. [D.] got upset and began spitting on the floor and walking to the door. . . . D. stormed out of the gym, slamming the door so hard the glass cracked. . . . K. and I escorted him to time-out, where we talked for about 3–4 minutes. I sensed that D. was really going to explode if kept in time-out. So rather than provoke a situation, I asked what he wanted to do. He wanted to go back to class and work. We went back to class, and he sat quietly.

In contrast to the foregoing incidents, in the three elementary school incidents that follow, time-out is handled well. It is swiftly employed in a businesslike (low attention to youth) manner for a few minutes, and it ends with the termination of the student's disruptiveness. Two features of Incident 32 are noteworthy. First, rather than employing what has been termed exclusion time-out, in which the transgressing youth is removed to another room, the teacher uses inclusion time-out, in which the youth is faced away from classmates but kept in the classroom (e.g., in a time-out corner). In this position, the student is denied the attention communicated by peers' facial expressions, gestures, and the like but can still hear the lesson as the teacher continues to offer it. Incident 32 also illustrates the effective combining and graduated sequencing of consequences as the teacher moves from warning, to time-out, to the withholding of privileges (also known as response cost).

(30) E. is not behaving in group (standing up, bothering other students). This behavior goes on after he is asked to stop. Teacher tells E. to go to time-out. He doesn't move.

Teacher stops group work, goes over to E., and escorts him to time-out. Then teacher goes back to rest of group. A few minutes later, after [the teacher] gets the other students started in next activity, he goes over to E. and asks him if he knows why he is in time-out. E. says, "Because I didn't do what you told me to do." Teacher says, "What are going to do now?" E. says, "Behave." Teacher then sends E. back to group activity.

(31) A teacher across the hall [had] a student who was crawling under the tables and over a desk and onto the window counter. I don't know how she got him to come over, but her class rule was that he would spend time-out with me. Several of us have made this arrangement—getting them out of the atmosphere and away from the teacher who may be ready to blow—into an environment that is separate. . . . We use each other as time-out, a separation, just to keep our cool, to keep the class cool, because there is no place in elementary for us to send them except to an office that is very far away, and we don't know if both administrators are there.

(32) Boy is sitting in group being disruptive. Teacher asks him to stop. Disruption continues. Teacher quietly asks him to go to desk, sit at side of room by himself, facing away from rest of class (time-out corner). He objects. She quietly insists and walks him over to desk. He finally goes over and sits down. In about 5 or 10 minutes she goes over and invites him to rejoin the group. He does, and within half an hour he is disrupting group again. She again puts him in time-out and this time writes his name on the board. When recess comes, he does not go outside with rest of class.

We wish to end this examination of disruptive incidents and their management by considering, as we did for rules violation, the intervention most likely to yield benefits in this context. Alone or in combination with interventions considered previously, this procedure is "catch them being good" (i.e., the positive reinforcement of appropriate, desirable behaviors). Whenever possible, praise, approval, or other rewards should be given to those previously disruptive youngsters who begin to behave on task. A second valuable use of positive reinforcement is its provision to other, nondisruptive children in the class, who then may serve as models for disruptive youngsters to emulate. Incidents 33 and 34 illustrate the effective use of "catch them being good."

(33) Teacher begins to read story to group. One boy is pushing and shoving. Teacher stops lesson, looks directly at student until eye contact is established, says, "B." in "teacher voice" with "teacher look." Then [the teacher] turns to another group of students and says, "I really like it a lot the way you're paying attention to the story."

(34) Teacher announces it is time to clean up. E. starts to throw things in room during clean-up. Teacher goes over to him and stops him from throwing blocks he is supposed to be picking up. Asks K. (quiet little girl who is very carefully doing clean-up) to please hold E.'s hand and show him how to clean up without throwing things. She comes over and holds E.'s hand, takes him over to table, and they spend rest of clean-up time holding hands and cleaning up. . . . After clean-up they join rest of group in circle. Teacher thanks K. for helping E. and asks her to pick out the book for him to read to class.

Refusal

Teachers and administrators increasingly report defiant student behavior in schools. Whether in the form of simple refusal, belligerent rudeness, or demands for respect, such behaviors are being experienced across the country at younger and younger ages. In some schools and classes refusal has become so common that rather than adopting a zero-tolerance, "consequate-it-immediately" stance, teachers wait until a long string of refusals occurs before responding. Incident 35 is an example of such much-delayed consequating. Here, in-school suspension was put into effect after the student's eleventh refusal.

> (35) Refusal to sit down and work quietly, rude comments whenever I ask her to, constant talking across the room, asked 11 times to sit down and work quietly. Disruptive behavior yesterday also. Warned and refuses to cooperate, is disrespectful to me continuously.
>
> *Administrative response:* Assigned in-school behavioral intervention program for continuous disruptive behavior in art.

Incidents 36 and 37 are, we believe, further examples of the correct intervention, incorrectly applied. In Incident 36, a student in his third year with the teacher behaves in a severely belligerent, refusing manner, and the teacher's response is to plan a parent conference *if it continues.* Especially considering the teacher's long acquaintance with the student and his parents, an immediate meeting with the parents would seem appropriate. In Incident 37, the teacher employs an incentive system in which absence of inappropriate behaviors retains points and gains a reward (candy). We are strongly in favor of the use of point, token, level, or other classroom incentive systems—especially in classrooms experiencing high levels of aggression—but the particular approach employed in Incident 37 errs in two ways. First, its intent is to reward the absence of refusal or other negative behaviors, with no simultaneous, "catch them being good" reward for positive behaviors. Second, like any other economy, the cost-benefit arrangement must be tied adequately to the desired behaviors. Here the student is given permission to engage in four additional transgressions before he pays the price in lost candy.

> (36) [The student] is belligerent, has a chip on his shoulder, refuses to do his work, constant disruption of the class, will not follow rules, will not take off hat, takes time from others. Student is totally uncooperative. I want to see a parent if this continues. This is his third year with me.

> (37) K. was refusing to cooperate during a lesson. He was running around hitting people. I put his name on the chalkboard with five marks after his name. I told him every time he behaved inappropriately I was going to erase a mark. If he had one mark left at the end of the period I would give him a piece of candy. He tested me to see if I would really erase them. He lost two marks and was exemplary the rest of the period.

Are the consequences powerful enough? Although we certainly do not wish to urge overkill, or a sort of "death penalty" response to all student infractions, we do strongly subscribe to the view already expressed that low- or midlevel transgressions, if not swiftly and appropriately consequated, are encouraged to grow into high- level aggression. The student refusal and defiance in Incidents 38, 39, and 40 were consequated with a reprimand and change of seat in the first instance, the seeking of an apology in the second, and a warning in the third. We believe none of these consequences is strong enough.

> (38) [The student] will not cooperate—she will not close her mouth. She will not follow class rules. She laughs in my face and does as she pleases. I moved her seat.

> *Administrative response:* Talked with her with chance she will improve.

> (39) Extremely rude attitude almost entire class period. [The student] never shut his mouth when I attempted to speak about his problem after class. He was rude—refused to cooperate at all— said he didn't care, ad nauseam. He

smiled and laughed at it all and thought his behavior was cute—and "So what?"

Administrative response: N. will see you before the end of day to apologize for his rudeness.

(40) O. was rude and disrespectful to me and given a warning. She also refused to do my work. [Two days later] I gave her yet another warning because she wasn't doing any work, was mimicking my instructions and disrupting those who were working. Today O. came into class blowing bubbles, so I asked her to throw the gum away. She did so after telling me not to "get her going." Immediately, she popped another piece of gum into her mouth, and when I asked her to remove it she called me a "bitch." Her behavior is hampering the learning process of others.

More fitting to the seriousness of refusal/defiance and more likely to thwart the escalation of such behaviors is the use, respectively, of time-out, detention, and in-school suspension, as illustrated in Incidents 41, 42, and 43.

(41) Many times a day some students tend to show aggressive behavior not through fighting, but by words, actions, tone of voice, and lack of respect for peers and adults alike.

One of my students . . . often strives and thrives for attention. He has a habit of putting his feet up on the desk next to him. Almost every day I ask him very nicely to remove his feet. He usually complies. . . . One day during English class, I asked him to remove his feet from the desk, and, to my surprise, he refused. I asked him again, and, without any response, he did not. The speech/language teacher team-teaches English with me 2 days per week. She asked him a few times to remove his feet while I continued on with class. He blatantly refused her requests as well. I then quietly went over to his desk and told him to remove his feet or he would have to leave the room. He then left the room.

After approximately a 5-minute time-out, I asked him to come back in the class. He came in and did his work.

The student received attention by not removing his feet from the desk; therefore, he continued his behavior. Once he was removed from class, he was in isolation with absolutely no attention. At this point he would do anything just to be back in class, including doing what he was told.

(42) S. is at a point where he believes drawing is all there is to do in class. I asked him to put away his drawing, and he snapped, "Get your hands off my stuff." I asked him again, and he refused. I told him to leave the class, not the building.

Administrative response: Detention with [teacher] today.

(43) [The student] refused to do any work in class and was disrespectful and continued to disrupt the entire class. I told him to stay after for detention today. Refused to stay for detention. Tried to call home—no one could be reached.

Administrative response: Assigned in-school suspension.

The final refusal incident included here illustrates not effective or ineffective consequating, but the manner in which this increasingly common form of student aggression can rapidly grow into assaultive, dangerous behavior. This incident supports the contention that refusal must be dealt with swiftly, consistently, and with adequately powerful consequences.

(44) T. stated several times in the morning that he didn't want to be in school. During fourth period, we were in the home ec room, and T. refused to stay at his desk, saying that he wanted to be sent to the office. He broke the wood doorstop, touched items on the teacher's desk, in general constantly doing something inappropriate. T. kept saying he was going to do something big that would get him out of school. I remained behind as the class went to Room 77. When I did arrive, an assistant told me that T. was sent to the office for banging on the file cabinets. I went to the office to get him—he refused to leave but finally did. As he walked by me, he said to me, "You make me fucking sick." When we returned to the room, it was time for lunch. T. said he didn't want to go. I persuaded him that he had to go. As we were about to walk into the door of the cafeteria, he stopped and wouldn't go in. I told him to go in—he said, "You go first." I said, "No, T., you go first." I put my hand on his shoulder to direct him into the cafeteria. Since

we were in the middle of the doorway, those students behind us began pushing. T. came full force at me, swinging his fist. Mrs. M. was behind him and she stepped toward him, saying, "Don't you dare hit her." He missed my face by an inch. I told him to sit down and calm down. He projected his face into mine and tried to swing at me again, saying, "I'm not afraid of you." I looked him directly in the face and said, "Don't you hit me." He motioned toward me again with his fist up and again repeated, "I'm not afraid of you." I said, "T., I'm not afraid of you either—just go sit down." He turned, saying something under his breath. I walked into the office [and] told them about the situation. I went to the classroom to get his phone number. I met T. in the hall. He said he was going to the bathroom. I watched as he went in. When I returned to the room within 2 minutes, T.'s coat was gone, and he was nowhere to be found.

Cursing

Cursing directed toward teachers, administrators, other students, and other targets is a behavior being more and more commonly experienced by urban, suburban, and rural teachers from kindergarten through senior high school. Reports of cursing were frequently in evidence in our pool of 1,000 incidents. Just as Incident 44 illustrated the manner in which student refusal can quickly grow into assaultive behavior, Incidents 45 and 46 show how cursing can lead to more serious aggression.

(45) I was in my classroom, which was the resource room. It was about two doors away from the special ed classroom that this child was in, and I heard the teacher talking to him outside in the hall. The noise level was getting louder and louder. I poked my head out my doorway and noticed that the teacher was screaming at him and he was also screaming back at her. I asked her if she needed some help, and she said, "I just can't take this anymore," [then] she went back into her classroom and held the door while he was trying to get in. So I intervened by going up to him and saying, "You know, it looks like you're angry. Can you tell me what's going on?" And he got right into my face and started yelling and screaming at me, calling me every name in the book: "Keep out of this, you mother fucker" and stuff like that. . . . I just looked at him and tried to be calm and say, "You need to settle down because this is getting us nowhere." . . . Well, it got worse, and worse, and worse until finally I was just in his space, and he gave me a good shove and . . . took off. Well, he ran out of the building, and people were looking all over for him, but there was no sign of him. . . . About an hour later, they still hadn't found this child. . . . He came back to school to catch his bus. . . . When he got on the bus, the principal went on the bus and told him to get off the bus. He didn't get off the bus, so the principal physically

48

took him off the bus, and the bus left, which really got this kid aggravated. So the kid ran into the building. . . . As he was going through the school, he pulled one of the fire alarms, and one of the teachers grabbed him and they wrestled, and they both went down onto the ground. . . . The kid jumped up and started running towards the outside of the building, and I physically grabbed him and restrained him. The principal came over and said, "Bring him over into the kindergarten room." So we brought him into the kindergarten room, where the principal unfortunately put him in the closet and closed the door. . . . He started kicking the door and put his foot through the door. . . . The principal went and called the police. The police came and . . . said a few things to the kid, which definitely didn't calm him down. He was getting more and more pissed off, and they cuffed him and dragged him out of the building like a criminal.

(46) K. came to school at 11:00 A.M. instead of 9:30 A.M. She entered a quiet classroom, talking loudly. She sat at her desk without removing her coat and attempted to have a conversation with several students. I tried to ignore this behavior and continue with class because K. becomes vulgar and abusive when reprimanded. K. did not settle down. Finally, I said, "K., stop talking to the boys, take your coat off, and get busy." She said, "Shut up, fucking bitch. You don't tell me what to do." I did not reply. Instead, I wrote a referral. When finished, I asked K. to come with me. She said, "I told you to shut up, fucking bitch. I threw a book at you before and missed. This time I won't miss." Having said that, she picked up a book and threw it at me. I turned so my left side was facing K., put my arms over my head, and crouched, raising my left leg. The book struck my lower left leg at the site of a break which is still in the process of healing. The pain on impact was excruciating. K. then ran out of the classroom and out of the building.

In previous sections we stressed the need for swift consequating. Aggressive behavior not followed by negative consequences is likely to reoccur, as shown in Incident 47.

(47) I was monitoring the halls first period and locking the doors by the gym area and sending kids out. N. called me a "bitch" for sending them out and locking the doors. Near the end of the period, I was sitting on the stairs by the gym, monitoring the area, and I heard the door open. I got up to check the door, and I heard a student say, "You better not write me up, you fat little bitch," and then I heard Mrs. T.'s voice. I went to see if she needed help, and I saw once again it was N.

According to many of our incident reports, the contemporary secondary and even elementary school student is often preoccupied with receiving respect. Perceptions of being disrespected ("dissed") are a primary cause of all manner of aggressive mayhem. While remaining true to their own beliefs and standards about good teaching and effective classroom management, teachers will need to recognize this student preoccupation and factor its reality into their handling of student aggression. In Incident 48, tearing up a student's forged note was apparently perceived by the student involved as disrespect and responded to in the incendiary manner described.

(48A—Teacher) P., a pupil in Mrs. M.'s sixth-period math class, asked a fellow student, D., to write him an excuse so he could get out of class. I watched her write the note and give it to him. A few minutes later, he brought the note to me. I explained that I knew that the note was a fake and tore it up. P. became abusive to me, grabbed my glasses case and tore it, then tore up Mrs. M.'s lesson plans for the next few days. I called the office for help, and the vice principal was sent down. P. and I were chest to chest while I escorted him out into the hall. The whole time he was abusive to me with rather vulgar language. At one point in the hallway, he pushed me. I saved the excuse and lesson plans that were torn up.

(48B—Administrator) On Tuesday, March 3, at approximately 3:00 P.M., I went to a math class in Room 147 to investigate a disturbance. A student, P., was arguing loudly with the teacher in the hallway. P. was being vulgar and abusive. I escorted P. to the office to complete a statement. He told me he had been fabricating a note to be excused. P. told me that the instructor ripped up the note. P. responded by tearing the man's glasses case. During the telling of these facts, P. repeatedly used vulgarities such as "mother fucker," "fuck," and "shit." Also, P. lit a match in my office during this discussion.

In contrast to the preceding incidents, those that follow represent appropriately consequated instances of student cursing. Though the interventions used vary, each appears to be a sufficient match in potency to the seriousness of the student behavior involved. As noted earlier, "catch them being good" will enhance outcomes. It is hoped that in other interactions with these same students, appropriate behaviors are promptly and consistently met with teacher praise, approval, or other rewards.

In Incidents 49, 50, and 51, a prompt call to parents is the consequence for cursing.

(49) A. came in to school on Monday, May 23 at 11:00 A.M. He went to the gym with the class without any incidents. When he returned to the room at 11:30 A.M. I asked him to sit down and work on his math assignments. He refused to comply with my directions, which would not have presented a problem if he had sat down. Instead, A. commenced with an array of verbal abuse: "Suck my dick, bitch, I know your fat ass mother, white bitch, you're a whore and a tramp." I listened without making any retorts. Then I requested him to sit down. A. again did not comply but chose to leave the room without permission. He went to Mr. D.'s office. I called parent.

(50) F. had trouble adjusting to school this morning. After he entered the classroom he became very profane towards my teacher assistant. He then became a disturbing influence on the class. He left the classroom without permission, then went to the boys' lav, where he stayed until Mr. T. picked him up. Mr. T. had taken F. to the time-out room, after which [F.] decided to leave and run around the building. He then came back to our room and refused to do any class work. While I was cutting some cards in half for Mr. L., [F.] became abusive, calling me a "fucking faggot, nigger fucking asshole" and told me to suck his dick. "I'll write on

your fucking shirt, you asshole." The office was notified that F. was having some difficulty and would not leave the room either for Ms. D. or myself. Mr. D. then came to the room and ushered F. out of the room and into his office. I then notified F.'s family that he was having some difficulty and to come and pick him up.

(51) The student was running around the building, refusing all reasonable requests of his teacher. I approached him and asked, "What are you doing?" He responded, "Shut up, bitch, none of your business." I responded that he was my business and I needed him to sit down and tell me what the problem was. He refused and walked out the front door. After remaining outside for a few minutes, he came back inside. At this point I told him he had some choices to make—take himself to time-out and remain there until he was willing to cooperate with his classroom teacher or call his father and discuss the problem with him. He chose to call his father. After about a 5-minute conversation with his father, he said he was willing to go back to class and cooperate. His father stated to me and to the student that he would call back in 30 minutes to see how [the boy] was doing. The student returned to class and was OK for the rest of the day. This was a positive resolution for this student on this particular day. Many times this same behavior has resulted in my calling his father to come get him for the rest of the day, letting the student and parent know that this behavior cannot be tolerated.

Incidents 52 and 53 illustrate the use of in-school suspension.

(52) C. was involved with someone being called a "bitch." When asked to go to office, C. refused—when told insubordination leads to suspension, she said, "Fuck you" and left.

Teacher recommendation: In-school suspension.

(53) I'm a teacher in an urban middle school, and this was a problem in the hall with a student named U. U. was walking down the hall, and he grabbed a student around the neck and was pulling up on the student. I told [U.] he

had to take his hands off of this other student. He did so but then turned around to me and told me to get out of his face. I explained to him that it was my job to keep things moving in the hall, and he proceeded to tell me that I was sweating him and that he didn't need to move in the hall. A few moments later he appeared in front of my station again. Once again, he was not moving toward class. I walked over to him and told him that he needed to go to class. He told me to fuck off, at which time I told him that I would write him up for hall behavior. And he just made a face at me which said, Go ahead, see if I care. I did go to the office and did write up a referral on U. Two days later I received a copy of that referral in my mailbox and was told that he had served detention in the in-school suspension room the day before.

Incidents 54, 55, and 56 employ out-of-school suspension.

(54) F. was asked to go back to his seat to raise his hand. I was helping another child. He returned to his seat and said, "I hate that fucking teacher." I cannot accept this kind of language in my classroom.

Administrative response: Parent called, half-day suspension.

(55) When asked to put a rubber band down, student looked directly at me and replied, "Fuck you."

Administrative response: Two days suspension.

(56) [The student] continually talks during class, refuses to face forward in seat and pay attention, ignores all requests I make because I'm a student teacher. He therefore feels I have no authority and what I say can go ignored. He also called me a "bitch," which he denied when I confronted him as he left class. Ms. I. called him back, and he held his hand at my face and hers and refused to stop. Tried to talk to student. Moved his seat [to] avoid further disruption. Assigned detention—didn't come.

Administrative response: Out-of-school suspension.

Bullying

Bullying in schools may well be the most frequent form of student-to-student aggression. It has many faces: name-calling, intimidation, starting or spreading rumors, threatening, shunning, racial slurs, extortion, theft, or physical attack. In spite of its diverse manifestations, bullying is often hidden aggression—no fight to break up, no complaint from the victim, no referral to the office, no calling of parents or police. Its effects on its chronic target, the so-called whipping boy or hostility sponge, can be both severe and long lasting.

Bullies tend to be physically stronger than their classmates, as well as more impulsive. They exhibit low empathy and high dominance needs, and they behave in a broadly aggressive manner. Whipping boys, in marked contrast, tend to be physically weaker, withdrawn, and cautious and anxious in their relations with others, also exhibiting low self-esteem.

The incidents that follow exemplify this type of aggression. We believe Incident 57 illustrates too great a delay in reaching out to the youth's parent. The teacher in Incident 58 more promptly carries out this consequence.

> (57) [The student] walked past N. and knocked into his work and then tried to start a fight by saying, "What are you gonna do about it? You ain't gonna do shit." She walks around the room trying to bully and intimidate people all the time.
>
> *Administrative response:* Detention on Tuesday, September 22. If there is one more referral, will call mother.
>
> (58) I can think of one incident where a particular student, for reasons that are not entirely clear, had regularly been picked on by the other students in the class. . . . In this particular instance, the kid decided he was going to fight back, and so what happened was that the little kid walked over to one of the persons who had been persistently virulent

and promptly slapped him, then went back to his seat. The person who had been slapped . . . did not think [the kid] was worth pursuing, and the teacher informed the student who had been picking on the kid that [this] is the kind of thing that happens when you do that to people over a substantial period of time. And then in the wake of that the teacher went right on with class as if nothing had happened. [The teacher] then contacted both parents that evening.

The bullying behaviors in Incidents 59 and 60 are responded to skillfully by the teachers involved. In Incident 59, the teacher makes use of a positive reinforcer identified by careful observation of student choices. Psychologists call this the Premack Principle, named after the researcher who noted that, although commonly used rewards or rewards chosen from a "reinforcement menu" might fail, when one observes what a student chooses to do if given a free choice, that choice (in this case, playing in a large box) will likely be an effective reward. Incident 60 depicts bullying as a series of pushing events. In this situation the teacher correctly parallels the continuing transgressions with increasingly powerful consequences—talking it out, calling parents, referral to the principal, suspension.

> (59) E. is an extremely aggressive child who bullies other kids no matter what their size. One day I was having a typical day with E.—chasing him around the halls, preventing fistfights with other kids. [He was] being very disrespectful toward adults. But on this day another teacher, Mr. Q., had a large box he was going to use to make a large storybook on a trip we had recently returned from. I noticed that E. really found the box interesting, and later, when he was having some problems, I offered to make a deal with him. If he calmed down and ceased in fighting with other kids, I would let him play inside the box by himself instead of doing computer class.

> By noticing an interest, I was able to use that same interest in a crisis situation as a vehicle to change . . . behavior, hopefully for the better.

> (60) An incident that happened was [when students were] walking in line and coming down the stairs and a child

pushed another child in the back. And what we did was have the children talk to each [other] about what happened and come to an agreement about what happened—talk about matters of safety and how we could have done it differently. Then the parents were notified about the incident and told that the children would be removed from the room if it happened again. In the incident of it happening again, they would be removed for a short time-out, usually with the vice principal, and the parent would be notified once again. . . . For the third time they would spend an appreciable amount of time in in-school suspension for violence on another person. Our class is 6- and 7-year-olds.

The final incident in this section returns us to the cautionary theme that teaching can be a dangerous occupation. The battered-teacher syndrome is being reported with increasing frequency. We see in Incident 61 that not only other students may become whipping boys, but that teachers may also be vulnerable to such aggressive behavior.

(61) We played well for 15 minutes. Last game. I warned only 5 minutes left. U. threw cards up in the air, then K. did also. U. threw cards at me—K. did, too. I stated, "I don't want to pick them up. The game is over. Let's clean up so we can play this game another time." K. and U. continued to throw cards. K. leaned back on his chair against the door. I pressed the [button to signal the] office for assistance. Both boys screamed so the office could not hear what room I was in. U. turned the lights off. I requested that K. get off the door and attempted to open it several times. K. would not let me. U. refused to keep the lights on when I requested. K. knocked over my flash cards. U. threw a garbage can. Mr. H. entered. When exiting the room, K. pushed me.

Sexual Harassment

Sexual harassment by students of either other students or of school personnel is a type of student aggression whose frequency and implications we feel have been seriously underestimated. Sexual harassment is quite common; its potential for escalating to more virulent forms of sexual (and other) aggression is substantial. Sexual harassment may take the form of sexual jokes, gestures, or looks; the spreading of sexual rumors; flashing or mooning; intentionally brushing up against another; touching, pinching, or grabbing; and perhaps other behaviors. A substantial number of students, both boys and girls, report consequences of such behavior ranging from embarrassment and fear to difficulties paying attention in class or even attending school. As for other types of student aggression, means of interrupting and reducing sexual aggression are well worth pursuing.

In the three incidents that follow, sexual harassment between students takes different forms, but in each instance it is consequated by appropriately severe action—namely, suspension.

(62) During Project Adventure, K. was choosing to disrupt the class. He was asked to stop several times and refused. He eventually was made to sit out for a few minutes. After that he was still disrupting the class and made several sexual remarks to one of the girls in the class.

Administrative response: I would like to recommend a 1-day suspension for K.

(63) On April 22, S. was referred to the office for grabbing the buttocks of a female student. He left the office, stating, "Fuck this school." S. stated that he did not touch the student but that he had left the office and cursed out loud as he left.

Administrative response: Suspension through June 4.

(64A—Safety officer) N. . . . is very sexually explicit in his recounting of sexual adventures and often has his hands inside his pants. His classmates ridicule him for his apparent sexual obsessions. This morning he was chased and accosted by another student who alleged that N. had mooned him. N. conceded that he made sexual gestures at him. . . . The officer counseled N. that indecent exposure and sexual harassment charges could be levied against him if he did not cease his inappropriate behaviors. The officer further elaborated that [N.] would not only be censured by the court system but ostracized by his peers.

N. has difficulty dealing with his sexual nature. The teacher had reprimanded him earlier in the morning for manipulating his hands inside his pants. The teaching assistant contacted his mom to inform her than N.'s behavior had necessitated a suspension.

(64B—Teacher) L. and N. were sitting at their desks. . . . L. noticed that N. had his hand in his pants and commented on it. At this point both students were still in their seats. Someone knocked on the door. I turned to answer it. In the few seconds that I had my back turned, N. had stood up and shook his penis at L. and mooned him. . . . L. was very upset that N. had exposed himself to him.

Less common but still present in America's schools is sexual harassment of school personnel by students. The three incidents that follow were all perpetrated by one high school student over a 2-day period. A social worker, a nurse, and a teacher were his harassment targets. We include these descriptions to highlight the importance of swift and severe consequences for such serious behaviors: formal hearings, suspension, expulsion, or other steps. None of these steps was taken here, and thus the student's sexually harassing behavior continued unchecked.

(65A—Social worker) Wednesday afternoon W. and I were playing cards in my office. I had the door open with a chair against it in order for the door to remain open. My back was to the door, and he was sitting across from me. When I told him it was time to go, we both stood up. He walked to the door, closed the door, and shut the light off. At first I told him to turn the light on and open the door. He refused and came over to me. He put his arms around me in a bear hug and squeezed. In a firm voice I told him to let go and turn the light on. I had to tell him several times, using a stern voice, before he agreed to let go and turn the light on. I told him that his behavior was inappropriate and that I would not let him in my room again if he continued. I informed him that a handshake would be more appropriate.

(65B—Nurse) This morning W. came into my office, shutting the door behind him. I told him to open the door and report back where he belonged. Instead of doing this, he grabbed me in a bear hug and attempted to dance with me. I continued to ask him to leave and let me go. Less than a minute later the door was opened by another student, and W. released me.

(65C—Teacher) On September 27, I entered my office and found W. hiding behind the door. He turned off the light, grabbed me in a very tight embrace, and refused to let go for at least a minute. I calmly told him his behavior was very inappropriate and he must let go. He kept saying, "Give me a hug." I said, "No, it is not appropriate for teachers to hug grown-up boys." I finally got the light on, and he let go of me. He was obviously sexually aroused and did not seem to understand that he cannot attempt to gratify his sexual desires in a forceful manner.

Last spring, W. did a similar act when he turned my light off and, panting very heavily, came around my chair and grabbed my neck with both his hands. He said at that time that he could do anything he wanted with me, implying that I was helpless. I talked him into releasing me and reported the incident to the building principal. I consider him a definite threat to my personal safety.

(65D—Administrator) The Child Study Team, as part of the ongoing child study recommendations on W.'s behaviors, have reached the point where we believe that he should be placed on homebound as a last in a series of maneuvers to modify his behavior. These included the following:

1. Time-out procedures
2. Isolation
3. Suspension

4. Crisis counseling
5. Therapeutic group session
6. Termination of day
7. Exclusion

These measures have provided temporary relief, but we have found by past experience that the most effective means is a prolonged exclusion. W. appears cognizant of his actions but persists simply because it enhances his status amongst his peers. We hold the last effective card—that is, isolation from his peers. After his last return from homebound, his negative behaviors remarkably subsided. We cannot tolerate any measure that is less than exclusionary.

During the last episode, W. wielded a knife and threatened to inflict bodily harm on another student. It is important to note that when he is in such rages it requires in excess of five adults to deter him from harming others. We do not always have the available personnel. If we had not been able to mobilize quickly, dire consequences could have resulted. Any behavior not dealt with in a manner that is clear to him is taken as license to repeat.

It is, therefore, our conclusion that he should be placed on homebound and again we will look at what we can do to program for him.

Physical Threats

How might a teacher best respond to a threatening student, not only to reduce the threat and prevent its reoccurrence, but also to keep the threat from escalating into actual physical harm? The student restraint and containment steps described in the next chapter partially answer this question. In this section we wish to examine verbal, psychological, and administrative means for reducing the potential for harm. First, all of the procedures we have illustrated in connection with lower level expressions of student aggression are potentially appropriate here—namely, time-out, withholding privileges, in-school and out-of-school suspension, parent involvement, and, in extreme circumstances, police involvement.

Beyond such well-established approaches, what is a teacher to do? First, stay calm. The suggestion is easy to make, but remaining calm in the face of a threatening, perhaps enraged student—perhaps one much larger than oneself—is not easy. In part because of the real possibility of physical harm and in part because a threat is unequivocally directed towards oneself, it is natural for the teacher to take threats personally. However, if threats can be seen for what they usually are, posturing toward any authority figure who happens to be present, staying calm becomes more possible. Learning self-protective techniques like the ones presented in chapter 3 will reduce the possibility of being injured, thus increasing the likelihood of remaining calm.

In the first four incidents in this section, the responses of a teacher (Incident 66), a police officer (Incident 67), and two principals (Incidents 68 and 69) illustrate the value of calmness.

(66) In our classroom we have an 11-year-old boy who is highly aggressive. The child has been moved from school to school. . . . He yells, curses, and physically threatens children and teachers alike. The child got in my face and threatened to hit me, saying he wanted to kill me. I remained calm on the outside, telling him that he could do what he

61

wanted to but I have the right to defend myself, so think very carefully about the consequences. Fortunately, he cursed a little more and went back to his seat, mumbling. He did remain seated and regained control.

(67) On December 8 . . . one of the school administrators approached me. She asked if I could assist her because a student by the name of T. was just suspended from school and was giving one of the staff members some problems. . . . She wanted me there in case he got out of hand. As I was walking towards the office, I noticed a young . . . male who appeared to be upset and was raising his voice. I was told that this was T. As I walked towards him, I asked him what the problem was, and he went to go around me, telling me to get out of his face. I asked him where he was going, and he again told me to get out of his face. I told him he had been suspended and needed to leave the school. He said he was sick of our shit. I asked him if he needed to get a coat or anything and told him if he didn't he would have to leave the building. At this point he started to swear, saying, "Get away from me, bitch." I told him that I was a police officer, and that's when he became even louder . . . saying, "Fuck you, bitch. Put your hands on me. Hit me." I told him I didn't have to and he was leaving the building now. At that point he threw down his hat and kept yelling, "Hit me, bitch" as I walked towards him and he backed down the hallway. At that moment a male teacher came along and grabbed T. and told him to calm down. He kept yelling and struggling around, saying, "I'll knock you out, bitch" as the teacher held him. The teacher took him upstairs to get his coat and walked him out of the building, and I watched him leave the school grounds. At dismissal time the same day, T. was outside the front doors of the school. I called for a car in case there was a problem. T. was told that he was suspended from school and should not be on school grounds. He said he was waiting for a ride. I told him he would have to wait off school property. A vice principal told T. that coming back on school grounds when he was suspended would be another charge against him when he and his mother went for the formal hearing.

(68) During third period I was asked to go to the principal's office. Mr. X. was reinstating N. following his suspension. Mr. X. quietly explained to me that they were discussing a change in N.'s program. I agreed that the changes could be followed through with immediately. As we calmly spoke, N. began to get rather hostile. There was no reason for the provocation. It was quite evident that N.'s hostility was directed towards Mr. X. Mr. X. never raised his voice. He was quiet, calm, and direct when responding to N. N. got angrier and angrier and began to threaten Mr. X. He wanted to fight Mr. X. and said that he could kill him if they got into it. N. said that he could make one phone call and have Mr. X. killed. He could get his brother's gun and kill him himself. He repeated the threat [that] one phone call could take care of everything. He told him he would have Mr. X.'s wife and children killed. He also threatened Mr. X. by saying, "You better watch out when you get into your car." Mr. X. finally asked me to take N. back to class with me.

(69) I was teaching a ninth-grade physical education class when a student walked in, flopped down on the gym floor and said, "I'm going to kill the bald-headed son of a bitch." To my utter amazement this child was talking about our principal. My reaction was "K., do you want to tell Mr. C. what you said, or should I?" K. said, "I'll tell him—I don't give a damn." I took him down the hall and walked into the principal's office. I said, "Mr. C., K. has something to say to you about the 1-hour detention you gave him." K. looked Mr. C. in the eye and said, "I'm going to kill that bald-headed son of a bitch." Mr. C. very calmly picked up the phone and said, "K., call your mother and tell her to come take you home for the next 5 days."

Threats are often accompanied by high levels of anger and physical activity. The student is "pumped," adrenaline flows, perception narrows, and the possibility of rational conversation—or even the student's hearing your attempt at same—diminishes. Even though in earlier sections we have called for swift consequating, sometimes the best policy is to allow the student to retreat and calm down before discussing the threat, its antecedents, and its consequences. This strategy is carried out in Incident 70.

(70) A fifth-grade student had been sent to the office for some disruptive behavior. . . . He was screaming at the principal and called the principal a liar and told him he hated him. I was asked to sit with [the student] in the office because he had threatened to leave campus. This student was in my special ed class. He was so angry he made himself sick and started throwing up. His sister was on her way to pick him up. He told me when he saw her drive up that I better get out of his way or he would knock me out of his way. He also threatened that if he couldn't get out of the office he would jump through the window. The principal finally made it back to the office. At the moment the student saw him, he started screaming at him, telling him to get out of his face. His fist was balled up the whole time. He pushed the principal. Finally, after [we tried] to talk to him and calm him down, his sister arrived. We walked him out to the car to go home. The next day a meeting was held to discuss the incident.

Threatening statements from students can be powerful indeed. Incidents 71, 72, and 73 underscore that this form of student aggression is not to be ignored.

(71) On December 11, D. threatened a substitute teacher, Ms. T., stating that she would be in a coffin like another teacher. Ms. T. asked D. if that was a threat. D. replied, "No, nigger, it's a promise."

(72) T. came to speech class. . . . Five minutes later he walked out without permission. . . . I asked him to go back to class, and he refused. I asked him several times, and again he refused. He then lodged himself between the door and wall. I put my hand on his shoulder and said, "C'mon, T., it's time to go." He said, "Get your fuckin' hands off me." I then said, "T., you need to go back to class or I'll have to call the office." He pushed the button himself and said, "I'm not afraid of D." I said, "Well, you'll have to deal with him." He then threatened me several times, saying, "Your ass is mine after school. You better jump right in your van fast because your ass is mine." I had several witnesses. . . . When I told him he had to go to time-out, he said, "You'll have to suck my dick first."

(73) [At] approximately 9:00 A.M., E. came into my room, and I said good morning. He said, "Don't talk to me—I'll beat your ass. Next time I'll leave bruises." I told him that should he push me again or touch me I'd have him arrested for physical harassment. He said, "Wait until I get you on the street."

At times, the potential for harm following such threats is made greater by persons other than the threatening student. Such was the case in Incident 72 when the teacher understandably, but at her peril, touched the student. In Incident 74, the potential for harm is increased by the teacher's difficulty in accessing help. In Incident 75, the problem is more one of the teacher's perceived lack of administrative support, which results in her reluctance to communicate with other school personnel about the threat.

(74) B. stormed into my class, pounding on the glass of the door. He started screaming at me, disrupting my class, and I told him to be quiet and to get out of my class. He said, "Shut up, bitch—you're not going to write a referral for me and lie about me." I told him to get out again, and he refused but was screaming at me the whole time. I tried to move to the other side of the room to call the office, and he would not let me out of the corner of the room. He said to me, "You're not going anywhere." I tried to get out, and he blocked me in. When B. blocked me in the corner of the room, I tried to walk around him. His arms were out, and when I tried to walk around his arm, he pushed me back so that I could not move from the spot that I was in. He said to me, "No, I'm not leaving, and you're not going anywhere." He was scaring me since he was raising his hand at me. I finally got around him and went into the hall. Other teachers came to my room to see what the problem was since they heard his voice all the way down in the ESL class. Q. removed him from my class, and he continued screaming that "I want to talk to that bitch who wrote a referral on me." . . . His actions were beyond inappropriate . . . threatening to me and my class. He was definitely out of control.

(75) Teacher: This teacher was told by this student who had been uncooperative and disruptive that

he was just going to bring a knife on Monday and kill her. And this teacher . . . didn't say a word to anybody for most of the day, until finally by afternoon she had told another science faculty member who unfortunately tends to overreact. . . . In the meantime one of our . . . staff . . . had gone and talked to the teacher and given her some support and said, "Look, you can't just ignore this thing—you've got to report it at least to the building administration, and what you do beyond that I guess is your own personal decision." . . . I feel bad that any teacher would just not feel comfortable going to an administrator to say, "Hey, look, this kid just threatened my life."

Interviewer: What happened after the administration found out about it?

Teacher: Apparently, the student was dropped from that teacher's course.

Interviewer: The student remains in school?

Teacher: That's my understanding.

Finally, Incident 76 illustrates a novel teacher response to student threats when those threats are denied—audiotaping the student's responses.

(76) Teacher: This incident started with the matriculation of a new student, an eighth grader. . . . His father said that he had gone to another school, that he was a good student—said a lot of real positive things about the kid and said that the reason [the kid] was coming to this school was . . . to have the kid live with the father. And the kid did pretty good, and what would happen was that he would go and do a thing, do what teachers asked him to do, but at the very end when people were not in the classroom he would tell the

teacher something that was real threatening, like "I'm going to kill you" or "I'm going to beat you up." . . . But then he presented himself when he was sent to the office as "Oh, I didn't do this" and "Ask the other kids." . . . So I didn't know what to do because I had a few teachers saying that . . . this kid is very threatening and I'm scared. There was one teacher that refused to go into the classroom when he was there. . . . So what I did was I got a tape recorder and set it up so that I was taping things that started after the bell rang and right around the teachers' desk when he would come up. . . . I asked the teachers just to act normal, and then we did hear on the tape that he was threatening the teachers.

Interviewer: What would he say?

Teacher: Oh, "I'm going to kill you," "I'm going to beat you up," or "I'm going to beat your daughter up" or a family member. He was really into getting into the family, the teachers, their property, their car, and so when I confronted him, he denied it again.

Interviewer: How did you confront him?

Teacher: I had him come to the office and I said, "You know, I really know that you've been doing this," and he said, "Naw, they're lying" and this and this and that, "I'm really a good student," and when I played the tape, he went crazy. It's like he wanted to kill me.

Interviewer: What did he do exactly?

Teacher: Oh, he stood up and popped his fist back. Fortunately, there was a police officer that was coming to the school, and he seemed to be walking right in at the right time, so [the student] was handcuffed. So I called the father, and the father said, "No, that's not true, my son doesn't do this," and I said, "You need to come pick up your son. Your son is going to be taken to juvenile hall," and he says, "Now look it, you can't do that because you'll be sued. . . . My son does not do any of that." So the police officer transported the kid over to the father's place of employment with me. And I took the tape, and the father listened to that, and then the father opened up and said that the son was doing that at the other school in the other city. . . . The kid never showed up in school again—we never found out what happened to the kid or to the father.

Vandalism

Vandalism is a common and expensive fact of life in America's schools. In 1991, for example, 11 percent of America's elementary school principals and 14 percent of its secondary school principals reported serious or moderate levels of vandalism. Window breaking is the most frequent single act of aggression toward property in schools; arson is the most costly, accounting for approximately 40 percent of the total annual cost of vandalism. Who are America's school vandals? Most are 11 to 16 years old, as likely to be white as nonwhite, middle class as lower class and, at least for graffiti and similar acts, female as male. They often are youngsters who are chronically truant, frequently suspended, and commonly retained.[2]

Much is known about schools with high rates of vandalism. They tend to be places with high teacher turnover and low staff morale. Facilities are often old and obsolete, and out-of-date classroom management techniques are used, classroom rules and disciplinary policies are ambiguous, and administrative support for teachers is weak. In contrast, low levels of vandalism appear to characterize schools having low student dropout rates, high levels of teacher identification with the school, parental support for school disciplinary policies, and teacher avoidance of authoritarian behavior toward students.[3]

The incidents described here involve vandalism targets ranging from items as small as a book (Incident 77) to a major portion of the school building (Incident 81). Yet each has a lesson to teach us about the control or reduction of student aggression. In Incident 77, for example, we learn that even a student who has calmed down and is apparently compliant may explode into assaultive behavior if the person he or she perceives as being the incident's instigator reappears on the scene. In a very real sense, it's not over till it's over.

(77) F. would not do assigned class work. He was told not to write in the book. When I attempted to take the book from him, he ran around the room and then out the door

leading to the hallway. I attempted to track him down. When I returned to the room he was writing in the math book. I then retrieved the math book from F. He attempted to take it back. He swung at me, hitting me lightly across the chest area. I then restrained him and placed him on the floor. Mr. Q. and Mr. C. intervened and held F. until he calmed down. While I was obtaining breakfast, he broke away from them and ran down the hallway to attack me again. He was again subdued by Mr. Q. and Mr. C.

Damage or destruction of personal property must be appropriately consequated, as was done in Incident 78 by use of out-of-school suspension and alternative learning center placement. The victim's "justified" counteraggression was also consequated, though more mildly, as we believe is appropriate. What did not happen here—and what we assert should have occurred—is that the perpetrator be required to make some kind of restitution. Incident 79 does illustrate the use of partial restitution as a consequence.

(78) D. tore up, destroying, K.'s yearbook, which is irreplaceable. When D. tore up K.'s yearbook, K. threw his lunch at D.

Administrative response: For D., 1 day out-of-school suspension, plus 2 days alternative learning center. For K., alternative learning center.

(79) On February 3, T. put salt in teacher C.'s automobile gas tank. He admitted to doing this.

Recommendations:

    1. Suspension through June 3.
    2. Allow alternative education through the Student Support Center.
    3. Restitution for one-half of total damages.

In Incident 80, not only is the vandalism more serious, but attempts to thwart it result in a serious attack on a teacher. Note that this teacher's several attempts to secure assistance from the office went unanswered. We urge that *all* teachers have an effective, preplanned means of obtaining rapid assistance in emergencies. In some schools, an informal arrangement with a fellow teacher in the next room may have to suffice. Other teachers may require that someone be sent to the office to enlist aid. The unresponsiveness shown by the administration in Incident 80 is, in our view, an exceedingly serious breach of good faith and an excellent example of very poor school management. In the present era of increasing in-school violence, teachers need to know with certainty that, at all times and under all circumstances, their requests for emergency assistance will be met with speed and efficiency.

> (80) K. was in my room for speech therapy. We were using the computer. I was taking the disk out, and K. wanted to stick his fingers in the disk drive. I explained to him that putting his fingers in the disk drive would possibly break the machine and that it was expensive. He proceeded to put his fingers in again, and I told him again as I pulled his fingers out. He then put his fingers in and bent the inside parts (the computer is broken). I then said that he had broken an expensive piece of equipment, I needed to get someone to look at it, and . . . he needed to go back to class. He crawled underneath the table in my room and said he wasn't leaving. I bent down to talk to him, and he turned the table over. He then threw markers and other things on top of the shelf. I rang the office when he flipped the table. I was going to open the door and tried to grab him, but he started swinging and trying to bite me. He was too out of control at this point. I rang the office again. He then punched me in the face. I had to put him on the floor to protect myself. No one responded to the ring to the office, so I had to try to open my door. I got it open and called for help. K. was struggling, trying to bite me the whole time. He bumped his head on the shelf. The whole time he was swearing, "I'm going to fuck you up, bitch."

This section's final incident reveals just how serious vandalistic behavior and its consequences may become. Here, two youths virtually destroy a major part of the school building. On a more positive note, this incident also nicely illustrates the "can-do" spirit of school personnel and the student body, as together they work around the damage to get on with their lessons the best they can.

> (81) Well, it's really hard to say what caused the two boys to do what they did. Both of them are not what you would call

the ideal kind of student. Both of them had been in trouble with the law outside of school. . . . What happened was they broke in one night, and they totally vandalized the new wing that we just finished in our building. They got hold of a BB gun, or several BB guns, and shot out every plate glass window . . . that went to the outside. And then they broke into the library and knocked over all of the shelves. And then they went down into the kitchen and vandalized the cafeteria. . . . The staff, because of the mess that we had, wanted to call [off] school. But I said I wouldn't dignify the action or the people who did it with the satisfaction. . . . The staff all pulled in. . . . I said, "Get your kids in your classroom and let's just try to get class and school going as though it's a normal everyday situation." As soon as the first bell rang I got on the P.A., notified the students what had happened and what we were going to do and [told them] that the library would be closed that day and that the cafeteria would serve food but it would not be the . . . lunch that we normally had. . . . By 9:00 I had the names of the two boys who were responsible for the vandalism. The staff all pitched in and got everything cleaned up so that we could have lunch in the cafeteria. Our library was down for about a week. You can imagine the mess, having thousands of books scattered all over the floor. . . . The total cost was somewhere in the neighborhood of $20,000. . . . We contacted the juvenile authorities—had both boys arrested.

Out-of-Control Behavior

Out-of-control behavior is disruptiveness gone wild. It is the incensed student, flailing, perhaps yelling and screaming, almost impossible to calm, and often requiring restraint and intervention beyond that discussed in previous sections. As Incidents 82 and 83 illustrate, the possibility of teacher injury is substantial under such circumstances. In Incident 82, an out-of-control student bites a teacher. As described in chapter 3, if the bite is on a hand or arm, pushing the hand or arm further into the student's mouth will cause the jaw to release, and any resulting injuries are likely to be more minor. If the bite is elsewhere, pinching the perpetrator's nostrils closed will cut off the air supply and may cause the student to open his or her mouth. In Incident 83, a very skilled teacher overestimates her own abilities. Instead of leaving the out-of-control student outside of her room and seeking further assistance, she ushers the student into her room and, alone, seeks to bring him under control. Her efforts fail, and her hand is injured.

> (82) There was a child in my classroom who completely lost his self-control. On this particular day, the student began throwing tape recorders, turning over desks, and screaming at the other students. I walked over to the student [and] asked him to sit down. He did not. I continued to talk calmly to this student and placed my hand on his hands and began to help him sit down. Once I had him in the chair, I placed my arm around his chest, holding him in the chair. At that point, I sent another student to the office for help. During this waiting period, the child latched his teeth on my arm. I calmly gritted my teeth and held on. Most of the other students in the class were very frightened and hiding beside their desks by this time. After a matter of minutes the principal arrived and assisted me in removing the child from the classroom.

(83) On March 29, a fight involving R. broke out in the doorway of my room. Upon separating the two students, Mr. A. and I were able to get R. into my room and close the door. R., while totally out of control, using foul language, kept swinging at me while I kept . . . trying to calm him. He kept grabbing my left arm while shoving and swinging at me with his free arm. At one point he turned off my lights, and I had to turn my back on him, while being hit, to find the wall switch. At another point he lifted a chair, drew it back over his shoulder, and asked if I wanted this across my face, as he stepped towards me. I was able to talk him into putting it down. Upon arrival of Mr. L. and Mr. M. I was able to get out of the room. . . . They took over, calling for help from the police officer in our building. I then was taken to the nurse to put ice on my swollen left hand . . . and went to the ER at Community Hospital.

Chapter 3 provides specific guidance for restraint to minimize injury to oneself, an out-of-control student, or others at the scene. In order to do so, it is always desirable to have assistance. Incident 84 is an example of the effective working of such collaboration. In stark contrast is Incident 85, in which the principal peers in the door, sees the wild scene, turns around, and leaves!

(84) Earlier this year we had a student who was a handful. He was put into the classroom I was involved with. . . . He would sleep all day. He wouldn't respond to any type of work. He did what he wanted to. He was absent quite often. One day, I believe he had stayed out all night, and he came into class real late, and he was just very irritable. He slept for a while, and he got up and he would have nothing to do with any of our assignments that we offered him. At that point the teacher asked him what he wanted to do, and he told her where to go. And he started to get really upset, and he started throwing desks around. At that point I was watching him. . . . He was disrupting most of . . . the classroom furniture—the desks—and he was moving towards the door. And I didn't want him to go out into the hallway, so I . . . cornered him and kept him from going out the door. He's a rather large kid for his age, so I had to put him down. And I got on top of him, and I kept him still. I used my

legs to lock his legs, and I held his arms over on top of him. And I stayed there until I thought he was calm, but he got up again. Luckily, I had help from another assistant. And we got him wrestled to the ground, and we put him into a time-out room on the other side of the school. At this point we contacted the school counselor. She called one of his relatives, and we talked with them. . . . We decided it was good for him to go home. . . . We ended up having to carry the kid out of the school, putting him in the car and taking him home.

(85) The incidents occurred in . . . a self-contained special education classroom that consisted of all boys, age 13–17. One boy had called another boy a fag. This was a common thing for the boys to call each other names. They were all friends. . . . However, on this particular day this did not go over with one boy. When he arrived in the room after break, he slammed himself into his desk. . . . I asked everyone individually how break was. When I got to H., he lifted his head and he appeared dazed. His pupils were enlarged and glazed over. He jumped up and began throwing desks across the room. He screamed and yelled profanities at everyone. I sent one boy to the office for help. I moved everyone else against the wall. He threw a stack of books at the boy who called him the name and repeatedly said, "I'm not a fag." He then overturned my desk and several bookshelves. He threw everything that he could move. He blocked the door with his body to prevent our escape. When the principal arrived, he peered in the window and turned around and left. He called the police for help. (I didn't know this at the time.) When H. heard the sirens, he became more agitated and he grabbed a Coke bottle, broke it over my desk, opened the door, and chased the principal with it. He held [the bottle] to his throat. He then dropped it and ran out the door just in time to be tackled by the police, handcuffed, and taken away.

Out-of-control behavior may be injurious not only to its perpetrator and to school personnel, but also to other students. Potential or actual injury may occur through direct victimization (i.e., being the intended or accidental target of the out-of-control behavior), as shown in Incident 86, or via a contagion effect, in which other students join in the melee, as is the case in Incident 87.

(86) The class was seated and "taking 5." I told the kids to line up for lunch. As they lined up, for some unknown reason G. picked up his desk and overturned it. It hit T. T. went after G. Because of other frustrations and G. screaming at the kids, the whole class went after him. I removed the rest of the kids and stayed with G. G. tore up the room, screamed, hollered, etc. When the rest of the class returned, G. picked up a chair and threw it at another child before I could get there. G. immediately picked up another chair, which I took away from him with help from another student. Things calmed down. Without warning, G. jumped up and overturned the large table, which hit two other kids. G. was removed from the room before the class attacked him. G. came back into the room sometime later with "Give me my fucking shit." The entire class went after him.

(87) M. acted totally irresponsible as she ran wildly through the hall, inciting students to run and follow. . . . She screamed and waved her arms, leading the growing crowd of students to the site of a fight. She laughed and threw herself around in the crowd. As the crowd came pushing down a side hallway, she was clearly moving . . . uncontrollably, endangering those around her.

For the resolution of out-of-control behavior, we recommend not only the more potent consequences illustrated for lower level student aggression—office time-out (Incident 88), parent involvement (Incident 89), and out-of-school suspension (Incident 90). It is also important to draw upon an especially valuable tool in the service of aggression management, the teacher-student relationship. The teacher whom the child has come to trust, respect, and even like, who is a stable figure in an often unstable life environment, and on whom the youth can depend has a great deal of capital in the bank, as it were, when behaviors need changing. The teacher who sat with an out-of-control youth until he calmed down (Incident 91) and the teacher who persisted in talking it through with a second angry youngster (Incident 92) show the power of this relationship.

(88) Some difficulty in morning [with K.] verbally teasing other kids. Also refused to do math in afternoon and escalated his negative behavior to get out of the room

(talking out, teasing other kids). Office was called—Mrs. O. asked if I could bring him down to the office. At this point K. had run out of the room, coming back to the room several times to disrupt—he would open the door and turn off the lights, bang on the door and window, and throw things at other kids, becoming unsafe to others. I led him down to the office by the arm, but he resisted, kicking the closets as we passed them, and he also punched me in the chest. In addition, he was cursing out loud in the hall on the way to the office. He remained in the office area for the rest of the day.

(89A—Safety officer) While working . . . in the capacity of police officer on duty, I was informed by . . . Ms. E. that O. was out of the classroom without permission. At this time, this officer observed O. going into the gym area. . . .

This officer . . . observed O. standing in the middle of the gym area with a ball. At the time there were a total of two classes in the gym. . . . In the position that O. was standing, she was interfering with the class, to a point that the class had to be stopped.

At this time, Mr. D. . . . tried to escort her from the gym. She then began to fight with a student in the gym (K.). . . . At this point, the entire class started to throw balls at her in an attempt to get her out of the gym. At this point, O. attempted to go after B., age 7 years, by throwing a bowling pin at him, striking him. At this time, Mr. D. and this officer tried to restrain her, as she was now striking out at everyone within reach.

This officer, along with Mr. D., restrained O. on the gym floor. . . . O. was restrained on her back. While attempting to restrain O., both myself and Mr. D. were kicked by O. . . . She had to be placed in handcuffs. . . . At this point, she was totally out of control, and there was no reasoning with her.

After about 15 minutes, O. seemed to calm down. Her foster mother . . . had been called and had responded to school.

(89B—Teacher) The afternoon of Wednesday, May 6, at 1:00 P.M., O. followed K. into the boys' bathroom. I pursued her and tried to coax her to leave K. alone. O. refused to listen and proceeded to enter the lav and slap K. on his head. Finally, I was able to escort her out of the boys' lavatory. O. continued to roam the halls as I followed. I encountered P. X. and requested assistance with O., who had now entered the gym area. Upon entering the gym, O. once again sought K. Mr. D. escorted her out of the gym area when O. abruptly turned around and reentered the gym. The class became frustrated with the constant interruption . . . and began to throw balls at O. O. became violently enraged and placed K. in a headlock as she dragged him across the gym into the office area. Simultaneously, she was kicking and striking other students with her free hand and leg. . . . O. then began to throw pins at the reminder of the class. P. X. and Mr. D. had to restrain her. . . . She kicked both of them. It was then necessary to place her in handcuffs. She continued to kick and scream out obscenities while in handcuffs. Mr. H. entered and requested that her foster mother be summoned immediately. I called her mother, who arrived within 10 minutes.

(90) We had a situation in the beginning of the school year with a 5-year-old kindergarten child—a boy. He was very aggressive once his mother left him here for the day. He had to be restrained because he was overturning chairs, trying to overturn a table, trying to leave the room. What was done was [that] the teaching assistant sat with him, restrained him so that he wouldn't hurt himself or someone else, while the teacher took over the rest of the classroom. We eventually had to call in the assistant principal to help us because the child was trying to leave. During the week we had the same situation most every day. Twice in 2 weeks he tried to go out of a window and had to be restrained. Eventually we had to have him be out of school so that he wouldn't cause further problems.

(91) As class was dismissing to go to homeroom, K. intentionally pushed (with shoulders) another student into the lockers. Words then ensued, but the other student quickly ran away from K. and into the back corner of the class. K. went after him to fight. The two of us teachers

interceded by going to the doorway to ring the bell for the office and stop K. from entering the classroom. K. pushed us out of the way several times in an attempt to get to the other student, who had gone to a back seat. [K.] was clearly out of control and had brought previous anger into the class (from breakfast). At the beginning of the class we had offered to take him out of the room for individual help, but he refused and was obviously already . . . angry. Then Mrs. N. and I had asked if he wanted to go to the office to talk—he refused: "Why? You ain't going to help me anyway. Nobody wants to help me. I already failed—why should I come to school?" etc. . . . I sat next to him the entire first period, during which he could do nothing because I felt he would be looking for a fight. He was extremely . . . angry.

(92) You could really deal with N. He was really intelligent. He was fair. He would admit when he had done wrong. He would apologize. What he wouldn't do was accept the principal getting in his face. And Mr. D. continued to do it. And as many times as I tried to talk to my principal about it, he wouldn't buy it: "He's a thug. He's no good. He's not going to make it." He had the kid pegged. Well, an extreme example of what happened to N.—last year, it was probably midyear, I was off doing something else when the principal came and literally grabbed me by the arm: "I just threw N. in your office. He is totally out of control. You have 15 minutes to get him under control, or he's being arrested." And then he parked the police officer outside my door. So here I am with this very agitated, angry young man, with a police officer outside my door. And I thought, Well, this is a hell of a position to be in. I will admit that this was the first time I felt afraid, because N. was so angry—his eyes were bloodshot. . . . And I went in that room fearful because I did not know what was going to happen with N. All I had to bank on was our relationship—that N. had some respect for me, that I had always been fair to him in the past. And N. sat there pounding his fists, screaming, "I'm going to kill the son of a bitch. I'm going to kill the mother fucker." And I had to let him go through all that acting-out stuff to bring him down. And the first thing that I got N.

to promise, and this was only a promise based on our friendship, was that he would not leave my office. Because I was afraid that if he bolted somebody was going to be seriously hurt and N. was going to end up in jail. And I was able to get that promise from N. that he would stay in the chair. And I trusted him enough to know that he would stay in it. . . . In the course of talking to N., I also found out that his brother had been arrested the night before in a drug situation, and N. is extremely close to his brother, and that was very upsetting to him. . . . I got him to calm down to a certain extent, but not calm enough where I could let him out of the room. And the only thing I had left to work with was calling his mother. I knew his mother, and I knew the power his mother had over him. I was able to reach his mother at work, and I didn't ask, I didn't beg, I told her, "You either come to school, you leave your job—I know you're at work—but you either leave your job and come now, or you're going to be picking N. up at the police station."

Out-of-control behavior is often difficult behavior to change. The student is "pumped up," frequently not mindful of potential consequences. The contagious arousal and aggression of others may make matters even more difficult to bring under control. As is the case for fights, illustrated in the following section, use of a combination of interventions may be the most effective strategy for out-of-control behavior. Though the incidents in the present section illustrate the separate use of a version of time-out, parent involvement, out-of-school suspension, and reliance on the teacher-student relationship, this type of situation may require that all of these interventions (and perhaps more!) be used simultaneously.

Fights

From horseplay to out-of-control behavior, the sections of this chapter to this point have primarily concerned aggressive *prefight* behaviors. Our consideration of the interventions in response to these behaviors has focused on their overriding goal to reduce aggression and, ultimately, prevent fights. When for whatever reason such interventions fail, are put into place too late, or are not used because a given conflict has no apparent precursors, a fight takes place and must be stopped.

In this section we will present a number of fight incidents and examine them for their potential lessons. Before doing so, however, we wish to offer a schema for fight scene management that we feel will help place the incidents and their lessons in a meaningful sequential context. This schema, outlined in Table 2, captures what we believe—from our own classroom experience, the responses of teachers interviewed, and relevant educational literature—to be fight management state of the art.

1. Make a quick assessment

Competent fight scene management begins with a rapid appraisal of problems and resources: Who is fighting? How many? What is their size and gender? Do I have a positive (or negative) relationship established with any of them? Can I see any weapons? Are there likely to be hidden weapons? Are there objects at the scene that can be employed as weapons? Is there an audience of other students? How many of them are there, and how likely are there to be joiners, goaders, or restrainers? Is assistance present? Available? Callable?

2. Call for help

We urge that the call for help come as early as possible in the fight management sequence. In many, perhaps most, instances, the teacher's natural, protective inclination to interpose herself or himself between the disputants, or to grab, restrain, or otherwise physically

81

TABLE 2

Managing the Fight Scene

1. Make a quick assessment.

   Consider disputants, weapons, need for assistance.

2. Call for help.

3. Use defusing tactics.

   Model calmness, talk softly and slowly, call students by name, use requests or distraction.

   Avoid threats, ridicule, running, physical proximity, interposing self between students.

4. Separate students *only* if you are skilled and safe.

5. Control crowd.

6. Interview disputants.

7. Take appropriate action.

   Consider counseling, mediation, referral, suspension, call to parents, call to police.

8. Debrief class.

9. Care for self.

---

intervene should be resisted until help arrives. We recommend delay with some reluctance because we realize it will often result in greater injury to students. But responding quickly and without support will only serve to increase the number of battered teachers in the United States. It is hoped that your school has in place a pre-planned, rehearsed, and rapid means for summoning assistance to a school fight scene.

3. Use defusing tactics

If aggression is contagious, so too is calmness. In the heat of the aggressive moment—especially if the aggression is directed toward oneself—it can be difficult to remain calm, speak slowly and softly, and move deliberately. But such behaviors displayed by the teacher or other school personnel at a fight scene can help defuse aggression. Models of calmness can engender calmness in those interacting with such persons. This effect is especially likely the earlier in the fight such behaviors are employed—before the youngsters involved are highly aroused. Additional defusing tactics that may be profitably employed are avoiding threats, ridicule, and "getting in the student's face" and instead calling the student by name, offering reassuring or face-saving advice, and making firm requests rather than demands.

4. Separate disputants *only* if you are skilled and safe

As noted earlier, we urge strongly that teachers not automatically assume that they must interpose themselves between two or more fighting students in an attempt to break up a fight. Teachers *do* get injured, sometimes quite seriously, and even though delaying restraint attempts until sufficient assistance arrives may result in additional injury to the disputants, such is often the best choice. Even with assistance, interventions should be attempted only if the staff possess the requisite physical intervention skills, as described in chapter 3.

5. Control crowd

Other students will typically be present or gather at the scene of a fight. Some may urge on one or more of the participants or actually join in the fight. Others will simply watch. Some will be frightened and intimidated. All members of this audience—fighters, inciters, onlookers, or others—are in danger of physical harm. Both for their own sakes and for those of the original fighters, any observers should be dispersed. As for the fight itself, swift and competent management will require the services of other, and perhaps several, school personnel. We urge that schools have in place as part of their call-for-assistance system an "all come code," by which all available school personnel may be summoned to the fight scene.

6. Interview disputants

This is the information-gathering phase of fight scene management. Ideally, each fighting student is removed by one—or better two—

members of the school staff to separate offices. During this shep-herding process, staff engage in whatever restraint and calming tactics are still necessary. The interviewer, typically an administrator, will ideally model calmness during the interview, thus encouraging con-tinued deescalation of fight-associated emotional arousal.

7. Take appropriate action

Consequences are determined on the basis of interview infor-mation, school policy, the participants' previous behavior and behavior during the fight, the extent of any injuries, and other consid-erations. Actions taken may include counseling, mediation, referral, suspension, a call to parents, a call to police, or any of the other inter-ventions illustrated throughout this text.

8. Debrief class

Other students in the class or school may be frightened after witnessing the fight, fearful of attack on themselves, or anxious about existing in a sometimes out-of-control environment. A brief post-fight opportunity for ventilation, reassurance, and clarification will be well worth the time invested.

9. Care for self

Student fights also provoke teacher anxiety and fear, and though very few schools provide opportunities for teachers to process such experiences, we urge teachers to make efforts on their own if neces-sary to deal constructively with the emotional consequences of managing student fights.

Student fights may happen at any time and at any place, but some times and locations are more common than others. March is the peak month for student aggression in the United States.[4] Teacher lore suggests that Mondays and Fridays, as well as the class periods just before and after lunch, are particularly fight-prone times. As Incidents 93 and 94 illustrate, the day before a holiday may be especially volatile.

> (93) It was the day before Christmas vacation . . . and this
> was a senior English class. . . . As the class went through
> there wasn't anything unusual going on, but as soon as
> the bell rang and the students got up to leave, one of the

basketball players, who is about 6'6", grabbed the boy who was sitting in front of him, who was also 6'2" or 6'3". And the first I became aware that there was a problem was that they had flung themselves through the air, landed on top of a student's desk, turned it over. And the one boy that seemed to be the aggressor picked this other kid up, and then they flew back across over the top of my desk and slid into the wall. . . . The boy's name was K. And K. had this kid's head locked under his arm and he was ramming [the kid's] head into the wall. Well, I have an intercom in my room, and I had immediately hit that and called for the office. . . . [Due to] the noise of the fight the kids were piling into the room, but it was so violent that even the kids were afraid to get close to them. And I remember that I was standing right next to K. this whole time, and it was like I was screaming in his ear. I was holding onto him, and he was holding onto this kid, ramming his head into the wall. . . . And then three administrators finally came in. And they finally, at that point, were able to pull K. off. . . .

I was scared to death that he really was going to kill this boy. When they finally got him to let go of this kid's neck, it was like he kind of just shook his head, and it was like he had lost control. My room was just a total shambles. . . .

How it affects me to be that close to physical violence [is] that once it was over and they were gone, it was like your knees start shaking, and it's like you can't let go of it right away. . . . I thought that I could just pull it together and get the room back in order and start teaching, but it took about 5 minutes for me to realize that I could not just go on as if that thing had not happened. [I.] had to call down and ask for someone to send somebody up to stay with the kids because I just had to get somewhere to get quiet, and quiet myself, and get myself back together after that was over with. And it takes a while to do that. I took the rest of that period just to kind of collect myself and try to be calm enough to go back in to then teach the next hour that was coming in. It was a frightening experience.

(94) On the day before Christmas holidays began, most of the high school students were restless and noisy. This is not

unusual before a holiday. In the narrow hallway and
between classes, a white boy (who defines himself as a
"head-banger") and a black boy (a star football player) got
into a shoving match. The black student was much larger
than the white student. I knew both boys fairly well.
Several black boys were goading their friend into fighting.
The two boys had squared off, and words were exchanged.
I stepped between the two boys, facing the black boy and
with my back to the white boy. The larger boy was very
angry. I spoke to him very quietly so that his friends could
not hear me and put my hands on his arms. I told him to
think about the consequences, to let it go. Then I walked
him to his next class. Then I fell apart and cried.

Not all school locations are equally likely to be the site of student altercations. Though most of the school day is spent in classrooms, classrooms are not the leading fight locations. As compared
with the locations where most fights occur, classrooms offer the
teacher greater surveillance opportunity. In addition, time is more
highly structured and less opportunity exists for incidental bumping, staring, and similar fight-inducing "dissing." Three sites that
are particularly fight prone offer less opportunity for surveillance by
school personnel and more opportunity for an audience of fellow
students, less structure, and more chance for events that can be
perceived as disrespectful. These include the cafeteria (Incidents 95
and 96), the bus (Incidents 97 and 98), and the corridors during
class transitions (Incidents 99 and 100).

(95) During eighth-grade lunch on May 14 at approximately
12:50 P.M., N. and T. were having a verbal confrontation
regarding a certain seat in the cafeteria. They exchanged
insults, and I was in between (N. was seated, and P. was
standing). Suddenly, they started to go at each other. I tried
to stop them. Another student tried to hold N. back, and I
tried to hold her down, but she . . . kept hitting me. D. G.
held P. back and the other student ran to the office.

(96) The episode that I want to talk about happened in a
high school cafeteria. I was on lunch duty and standing near
the lunchlines as the students were lining up to get in. The
line had just been allowed to go in so that it was moving

up rather rapidly to fill through the area where you pick up your food. . . . Two ninth-grade girls . . . had a confrontation, and there was a lot of shouting and screaming going on behind me, and as I turned around the first punch was landed. And I was standing behind . . . the puncher, and before she could land another one, I grabbed her arm and tried just to keep her away from the other girl. As soon as I grabbed her arm and held her, that was a sign for the other girl to start beating on her. There were no other adults around. What I had to do was to let the one go that I had and try to get in the middle. . . . Another teacher arrived, and actually a couple more arrived, and one girl was grabbed and subdued by one of the male teachers, and I took the one that was nearer to me. . . . I grabbed her by the left arm, and she hit me three times in the face with the right arm.

(97) Two students on a bus got into a serious fight, leaving a student injured. A fifth-grade boy got up and hit a sixth-grade girl on her arm because he and several boys were angry with her. She told him to leave her alone—he went and sat down. A few minutes later, the same boy got up, walked over and hit her arm again, and sat back down. She got up, walked back to his seat, gave him a black eye, and scratched up his neck and face. The girl's mother felt her daughter was justified in what she did . . . both students were suspended from the bus and school.

(98) I had an older student trying to beat up on a younger student on the school bus. I got on the bus and tried to prevent the kid from hitting the other student. Busses are tricky because you can't always get two adults on to break up a fight—there is not enough room. The kid was able to instead attack me. He pushed me out the door, and, as I tried to get back on, slammed the door on my arm. Well, things were not going well at this point, so I tried again. By now the police officer was on the bus by way of the emergency exit, and we were able to remove the student from the bus. We ended up handcuffing the student, and the officer placed him under arrest.

(99) It was during a transition between gym and some other class. The students were 16 and 17 [years old] and

had gotten ahead of the class after gym. By the time I got to the room they were in an all-out fistfight. Both students were my size and I was new, so I thought I could or at least should break up the fight. I reacted on impulse and learned from the school of hard knocks about breaking up fights. I pushed one kid off of another kid, and as I did this the kid on the bottom went to hit the other student and ended up hitting me, hard!

I was able to keep the two apart after that until help arrived a few seconds later. But I learned not to break up fights impulsively. They were mutual combatants. Both students wanted to fight, and there was probably no reason for myself to risk injury in this case. It wasn't like I had to protect a smaller child from the class bully. I should [have] waited for help to ensure everyone's safety.

(100) The part that was most upsetting was that something . . . like a lock was used as a weapon. . . . It happened when cycles were changing. When you get the mob congestion I think staff as a whole get very nervous because you can't get to the people who may be hurt, and you've got other onlookers, and the kids don't follow the directions to move on to get to class. . . .

Apparently, it happened in the bathroom and was carried out into the hallway. . . . The bell rang for sixth hour to begin, and so the commotion was going on, and the kids trying to get from here to there [were] blocked. Well, then everybody surged together to see what's happening, and that means staff people can't get to the scene either. . . .

I got in there pretty quick, and I saw the principal holding each girl by the arm to separate one with the left [and] one with the right arm. And he was talking to them for a minute, and I thought it was over, and then all of a sudden they started throwing punches again at each other, and I believe his glasses got knocked off in the process. One girl he let go, and she kind of went to one side of the hall, and the other girl kept fighting him, so he pushed her up against the locker and held her arm. He took his arm and held her against the locker up to her neck until she settled down. . . .

[He] basically never said a word and straightened his tie afterward, pushed back his hair, and that was it.

Student fights may be touched off by any number of events. In addition to time and place antecedents, precipitating events commonly include teasing (Incident 101), insults (Incident 102), cursing (Incident 103), racial slurs (Incident 104), bumping (Incident 105), and that particularly common, incendiary, and offensive provocation known variously as "mad-dogging," "staredown," "the 1,000–yard stare," and "stink-eye staring" at the other individual (Incident 106).

Teasing as provocation:

(101) Shortly after my class began, two students (boys) verbally began arguing over the detention and referral one of them had received. The referral occurred in the previous class. One student was making fun of the other's troubles.

A fight broke out. Tables and chairs were being pushed around the room. I tried to get between [the students]. They were not hearing me. I then told the others in [the] classroom to move out of the way. I told one student to push the buzzer to the office and say "fight." We didn't need to say anything—they could hear. Other teachers came over to see if I needed help. Some students from another class had to be told to go back. I let [the boys] fight until the principal and assistant arrived.

Both boys were bleeding from the nose. One's face was swollen. When they realized the principal was in the room, they broke themselves up.

Each was suspended 3 days.

An insult as provocation:

(102) We were having a birthday party for a 16-year-old girl. There were about nine students in the room, all about the same age. During the party we had one student who became jealous that this young girl was getting all the attention. He was a very violent 17-year-old, about 6'3" and of a moderate build. Anyway, he decided to disrupt the party by digging his hands into the cake and then eating

it. The teaching assistant became very offended, even more so than the girl (who was very intimidated by him). [The assistant] blurted out that he was a selfish pig and other comments that she felt were appropriate, and then it happened. The student attacked the girl whose party it was.

He grabbed her by the neck and pushed her into the window. Then he began slamming her head into the brick wall. This kid had threatened me many times and seemed to want to force a physical showdown between him and myself. I always managed to avoid this, but I guess this time I wasn't going to be so lucky. Since the student was so large and, given the immediacy of the situation, I had to act alone. I didn't want to get hurt or see the girl hurt, so I decided I had better be aggressive and protect her. So I placed him in a very hard headlock and yanked him away from her. I then used a modified hip throw to take him to the ground. This was dangerous. I wouldn't normally do this, but this kid was bigger than me and was seriously injuring the girl. I took no chances and when on the ground I kept him tightly in the headlock with a lot of pressure on the jugular area to prevent him from getting a burst of energy. I had to hold him for what seemed . . . a long time. Help came, and the fiasco began.

Three or four of us were now restraining the student, and it looked and sounded like a bunch of nonprofessionals. Everyone shouted directions and tried to talk to the student all at once—it was terrible. I felt one person needed to direct the restraint and that SHOULD BE ME. I was the initiator and was in proximity to talk to the kid. Anyway, one guy said, "He's not struggling anymore—I'm going to get off his legs," and he got off without consulting me. The kid was whispering that he was going to kill me. Then the principal said, "OK, let him up." I told them it wasn't a good idea. I let go, [the student] got up swinging, and it started all over again. You need a system for restraint and crisis management. People on the team have to be able to accept the lead person's decision.

Cursing as provocation:

(103) Two freshman students (females) became involved in name-calling and then fighting. The fighting consisted of

jerking earrings from the ears, pulling hair and clothing, and cursing. The emergency button was pushed to notify the office. The girls were grabbed by students to stop the fight. They were stopped briefly. Suddenly, one of the boys turned one of the girls loose, and they began again. By this time assistance arrived from the office, but this did not deter the action. [The students] were separated and forcibly moved down the hall to the office as they continued to attempt sticking each other and cursing each other.

Racial slur as provocation:

(104) Seventh-grade students were busy going to their classes. Teachers were instructed to stand at the door, and a seventh-grade girl (who happened to be white) was talking to her girlfriend. . . . With me standing at the door and those two standing at the door, we were blocking the doorway. So a seventh-grade boy (he was black) was going to get in the doorway, and he just kind of squeezed in between us, and the girl [used] a racial slur. She said, "Look out, nigger." And before I knew what hit, he was beating her with both fists. I think he was holding her hair actually with one hand and beating her face, and blood was everywhere. And two other teachers were standing at their doors, as I was, up the hall from me, and they were both kind of looking my way. And as this took place, they kind of turned around so that they didn't have to be involved. . . . I tried my best to pull him off of her. . . . Finally, another seventh-grade boy came and helped, and the two of us got him off of her. . . . So what happened is they both were taken to the office and put in separate rooms. They were both given the same amount of suspension, which happened to be 3 days.

Bumping as provocation:

(105) There are fights almost every day in school, usually over small, petty problems—for example, getting in some-one's face, saying something negative to someone, name-calling, boyfriend/girlfriend spats or jealousies, etc.

The . . . fight was right before the last period of the day. The halls were almost cleared. Two boys were walking to class in front of me. One boy was walking in the opposite direction, and I think someone bumped into someone else. Words were exchanged that were inaudible to me. All three boys stopped, and I could tell a confrontation was brewing. I stepped in between but to the side of the two boys eyeing each other. I encouraged the students to drop what was bothering them and keep moving to avoid getting in trouble. I told them if they both kept walking, there would be no negative consequences. Neither seemed too concerned about the consequences and avoiding punishment. One boy swung and missed. The other wrestled him to the ground. They were rolling on the floor when another female teacher came to help break up the fight. Finally, before any more adult intervention appeared, two students came, and each restrained one of the students. The fighters were still swinging at each other, and I escorted one of the fighters and his restrainer into the teacher's room to separate the two. An administrator then appeared and took the boy to the office. Both students were put on suspension.

Staring as provocation:

(106) It was Monday morning, and I was watching the students line up. . . . I noticed K. and P. staring at each other in a way that was abnormal and hostile. I rushed to intervene as K. grabbed P. by the head and upper body (it seemed like she was grabbing his jacket, or it could have been his entire upper arm). I first told them to stop, and when that didn't work I pulled P. . . . who was starting to strike back at K. . . . He had struck K. about three times before I could pull him away, while she was grabbing and striking him continuously. She started to go towards P., but another teacher assisted in pulling her away from the fracas also.

How can the teacher best intervene? Going it alone is very often a dangerous idea. Note in Incidents 107, 108, 109, and 110 how single-person intervention led to injury for the teacher or other school personnel.

(107) I was in a situation where two girls were . . . street fighting. I think it was over the boy that probably fathered

both of their babies. . . . They found out about it in the classroom, and it got very aggressive, very fast, and one of the girls was due to deliver within a couple of weeks. . . . And when they just got out of control they were getting real violent . . . very quickly. And [it] started to look like there were going to be some kicks to the belly and hair pulling and just things that could potentially damage not just the young woman but the baby. . . . I made the immediate decision to get in front of the two girls. . . . I stepped between one of them, and the other girl pulled back and grabbed a desk. . . . She raised the desk over her head or at least toward the back and actually just ripped it and it hit me in the back, and I went to the hospital. . . . That was really just another example of just basically making . . . bad choices. . . . When kids accelerate to the level of really a violent conflict, because so many of us haven't been . . . coached through what are the kinds of decisions that are better to make in those situations, we just react, and very often, I think, we react in ways that may not be the best for everyone involved.

(108) On November 4, a fight occurred between two students, E. and D. E. fell to the ground. At that time, L. entered the fight and kicked E. twice in the head. Dean of students, Mr. M., tried to break up the fight and in doing so was kicked by L. L. admitted to kicking E. once but denied kicking Mr. M.

(109) I had two boys begin a fistfight in the doorway of my classroom just as the bell rang for classes to change. I tried to get them out of the doorway. . . . I ended up getting knocked over my desk as the fight progressed. Even though the boys were not attempting to hurt me, I was getting hurt because I put myself in the middle and they were not willing to stop fighting. . . . Both boys received 9 days [in-school suspension]. . . . I went to the chiropractor for a series of adjustments and found out that the school had no insurance, workman's comp, or anything to cover the expenses. . . . The worst thing was that this happened on the second day of a school year, and it popped the bubble of renewed idealism that I had been able to build during the summer.

(110) During my first pregnancy (about 6 months along), I was teaching self-contained learning disabled students who were quick to anger and extremely deficient in self-esteem. Two of my boys who had words earlier in the day got into a scuffle in the hall outside my classroom door. . . . At the onset, I automatically and without thinking stepped between the boys. As angry as they both were, they just stopped. I don't know if it was because of my condition or because of me, myself. Regardless, I later realized the danger in which I had placed myself and my unborn child. I now wait for the fight to break or be broken.

In the schema for fight scene management we recommend first a quick assessment, then an immediate call for assistance. In the next two incidents, the teachers involved made such a call. Two intervenors were sufficient in Incident 111, but not in Incident 112, in which serious injury to a student—and legal difficulties for one of the intervenors—occurred.

(111) While [I was] teaching a fifth-grade math class, my door was opened by a sixth-grade student who yelled for me to come into the hallway because of a fight. I arrived at approximately the same time as the teacher across the hall. Two female students were punching, kicking, and pulling hair. Both girls were bleeding from the face. As I grabbed one girl from behind, the other teacher grabbed the other. I was elbowed in the abdomen. I pushed her into my room and behind the door, placing the door between the two of us. One of my students pushed the call button to the office to call for help. The principal responded immediately and took both girls, with assistance, to the office.

(112) The incident started when one student pushed another student into the wall. The student who was pushed punched the other student, which resulted in an all-out fight. I ended up getting involved by helping break up the fight. I restrained the kid that was on top, and a science teacher grabbed the student that was on the bottom. The student that I pulled off the top calmed down pretty quickly. However, the student the science teacher restrained kept trying to get away and fight. The student's struggling resulted

in both the teacher and him falling to the floor. When the student fell to the floor, he hit his head on the wall. The blow to the head caused the student to have a seizure. The student I restrained went to the office and got suspended. But the other student ended up going to the hospital. I had this strange feeling that this wasn't going to be the end of this incident. I had a sense that, because a teacher was involved when the student had the seizure, there were going to be repercussions. My feeling was correct because the next day the parents of the student came in and filed charges against the teacher. It wasn't the teacher's intention to cause the seizure, but the parents didn't want to hear that side of the story.

This incident really makes me think whether or not I should break up fights at school. I have always been willing to perform this function, but now I just don't know. I really believe that if the school administration doesn't stand behind this teacher, there will be no teacher willing to step in and break up a fight. I am unsure I should put myself between two students when my career could be in question.

In Incident 113, four staff members were required to break up a fight between two students—two restrainers per student. Incident 114 illustrates the use of an "all-come code" to signal all available school personnel to the fight scene. Use of such a code is strongly recommended. In a real sense, one cannot have too much help in managing a fight.

(113) This is an incident that occurred at an urban middle school between two seventh-grade girls. At seventh period, the end of the day after lunch, N. and T. were quietly working at their desks, having a quiet conversation. The rest of the class was being rather noisy, as they had been all week. Things started to settle down, and an administrator came in to check and find another student. While she was talking to me things were pretty quiet. The moment she left, however, T. stood up, and then N. stood up, and they started to fight. They grabbed each other—they were kicking each other and screaming and pulling hair. It took four adults to separate the girls. While they were fighting, the

class was standing around cheering them on. . . . After the students were separated, T. was taken to the office. Two of us held N. so that she wouldn't run after T. [N.] was so just completely out of it, just saying, "Let me go, let me go, let me go after her." . . . N. was very difficult to calm down. . . . N. was suspended out of school for 3 days. . . . T., on the other hand, has a very full, full folder. She has already been to a formal hearing. . . . She will in all probability be sent to the alternate school.

(114) Well, it was an incident that happened at a skating rink one weekend, and these two young fellows brought it to the high school. And apparently during their lunch hour it escalated, and they got into a fight. And at the high school we have a certain code when there is a fight. We sound that code number, and that's a code number for all the administrators to report to the cafeteria. Well, since my office is on the first floor, I was the closest one to the cafeteria, so I got there first. And when I got there, these two boys were fighting, and the kids were gathered around and hollering and carrying on. And the young man that was losing, more or less, I grabbed him.

A particularly troublesome and often dangerous aspect of fight scene management is that, at times, those we would like to pitch in (other school personnel) opt not to, whereas those we would like to stay away (other students) arrive in droves. In a number of the incidents reported (e.g., Incidents 85, 104, and 142), school personnel chose not to become involved in helping a teacher break up a fight. In Incident 115, even an experienced teacher remained passive.

(115) A fight erupted at recess between two female sixth-grade students. Other students immediately formed a ring around the fighting students, calling out encouragement to them. I ran to the scene, blowing my whistle all the way. I moved through the group of students ringing the fight. The other teacher on duty followed behind me. The girls fighting were totally out of control. The other teacher made no move to separate them. I knew in this situation that stepping between them was not a sensible action, so I got behind the one I thought would be easier to calm down,

waited my chance and, when it came, wrapped my arms around her from behind, pinning her arms to her body. I lifted her bodily from the group, turning my back to the other fighter to shield the student I [was] holding, plus hopefully myself, from the blows of the other student. [I] started walking as quickly toward the office as I could, talking quietly and calmly to the girl as I went in an effort to calm her. She responded to me, and, about halfway to the building, I was able to let her walk with my arms still around her the rest of the way to the building and to the office.

The other student, left with no one to fight but still in a state of rage, was eventually talked into walking to the office with the other teacher.

I am still bothered by the fact that the other teacher— a veteran of 20 years—took no action, forcing me—a second-year teacher with far less experience—to make the decision as to what action to take and then to carry out that action.

Keeping other students away from a fight scene is often very difficult because there are many of them, few of you, and most of your attention must of necessity be directed to the altercation itself. Potentially inflammatory audience effects were handled effectively in some of the incidents already presented: speaking softly to one or both disputants so those watching cannot hear (Incident 94); sending the audience away in a directive manner (Incident 101); permitting one or more students to help break up the fight until other school personnel arrive (Incidents 103 and 105). Rewarding those students who help break up a fight or at least do not urge its continuance and punishing observers who encourage the fight or who actually join in a fight are also legitimate strategies.

The final step in effective fight scene management is debriefing for observing students and the teachers involved. We find it unfortunate but not surprising that, although there were a few examples of student debriefing in our 1,000–incident pool (e.g., Incident 116), there was but a single report of postfight attention to a teacher's *own* emotional needs (Incident 93). With that single exception, teachers did not mention that they "had coffee with colleague to talk it over," that "the principal sat me down in teacher's lounge and offered a sub for a period or two," or that "I left early that day to pull myself back together." Quite the contrary, teachers commonly noted that they "resumed class" or "got ready for my next class period." For the teacher's own emotional health and career satisfaction, as well as for sound educational reasons, postfight teacher debriefing is an exceedingly important final step.

(116) This is . . . an after school program for 14–18-year-olds. . . . We saw eight boys around the weights. All of a sudden [there was] a loud commotion, with the boys jumping back and two engaged in a struggle. We responded—directed both boys to step back. After the second request they did. We told one to go to front office and other to go sit on couch.

[During the] interview, one boy [was] extremely frightened, upset, and crying—stated altercation had begun when other boy jumped on him and began choking him. No clear cause or reason why—boy that was choked hadn't provoked it. . . . Explained to other boy that he had broken a rule about committing a violent act on another. This wouldn't be accepted or tolerated. The consequence was what the kids had laid out earlier in the year—he would be suspended from program beginning now. . . . We liked him and felt he offered a lot to the program, but he needed this time to consider his behavior and learn new ways of dealing with his temper. He agreed and went through 3 weeks of counseling and reentered program.

Called a group meeting with everyone—explained B.'s suspension and reasons why . . . his choices were his to make. Asked if there was any discussion of it and told kids it was over and we would be reliving it over and over with constant talk.

Attacks on Teachers

A few decades ago, the probability that a student would physically attack a teacher or other member of the school staff was very close to zero. Now attacks are a sufficiently frequent event that teacher self-protection articles and manuals proliferate, an increasing number of school districts are providing their personnel with self-defense workshops and equipment, and one finds in writings about schools increasing reference to the battered teacher syndrome. The restraint and containment training that constitutes chapter 3 of this book also reflects this growing, and apparently necessary, educational preoccupation.

As with the forms of student aggression examined earlier in this chapter, consequating of student attacks on teachers must be swift, consistent, and appropriate to the seriousness of the student behavior. In Incident 117, the sequence of events graduates from a warning, to name on board, to a calming attempt, to day termination, and then to suspension as the student's assaultiveness progresses. In contrast to this instance of appropriately graduated consequating, the teacher in Incident 118 does relatively little as the student progressively ignores her, kicks her, curses her, and "swats" her with papers. *Then* the teacher requests help. Similarly problematic are teacher interventions that are swift but inadequate in potency to the seriousness of the aggression. In Incident 119, the youth forcefully attacks two teachers in several different ways and is placed, as a consequence, in time-out. Interestingly, the time-out procedure is used in this incident twice (even though it proves inadequate in its first usage), both times incorrectly. Time-out is appropriately used for a few minutes as a calm-restoring placement away from the opportunity to receive the reward of attention for inappropriate behaviors and not, as used here, as a place to put the youth "for the rest of the day."

> (117) Student was causing a severe disruption. He was
> given a verbal warning, asked to allow the rest of the class

to continue with the lesson, asked to just be quiet so teacher could continue.

Teacher continued. Student continued to speak out, making rude comments about other students, teacher, etc. Finally, teacher put student's name on board.

Student rose from his seat, became enraged—shouting obscenities, moving toward the teacher. The teacher moved behind her desk and put some space (desk) between her and this 16-year-old. Two other boys stood up to protect the teacher. She waved with her hand for them to stay seated.

The student stopped and was shouting, face red. The teacher tried to calm the student by restating an earlier offer to talk after class. "You sound upset—let's just sit down and talk." Student responded, "Fuck you" and began to throw things at the teacher. The teacher dodged and caught some of the stuff. The student was leaving the room. Classmates tried to stop him. The teacher said let him go.

The student left the school grounds and got 3 days out of school for punishment.

(118) K. left his classroom at 10:45 A.M. to attend speech. As soon as we were in the room he went to work. . . . Another student showed up at the window and started cursing. . . .

I told K. to ignore him, and K went to open the door. "K., do not open the door—ignore him, and we will finish our work." I said this three times. K. opened the door. I tried to physically close the door, and K. kicked me in the shins. . . . K. sat back down. . . .

K. remained seated and started swearing at me. . . . He got up and went to open the door and then pressed the buzzer for the office. He swatted at my face with the . . . work. . . . I pushed his hand away to protect myself from the papers, and I put my hands in front of my face so he wouldn't hit me anymore.

I requested help from the office. Ms. T. walked by to get Mr. M. . . . At that point K. smacked my face, pulling my glasses off of my face.

(119) Around 12:10 P.M. M. was walking around the room arguing with another student. I asked him to sit down and finish his lunch. He picked up his milk and threatened to throw it on me and another student. I again asked him to sit down and drink his milk or his lunch would go into the garbage. He threw [part of his lunch] away and went to his seat and picked up his soup. Also, he again threatened to throw [the milk] on me and the other student. He went over to the garbage and, instead of throwing [the milk] in the garbage can, he threw it at the wall. I told him that he needed to clean it up, and at this point he began swearing at me. . . . I then took his arm and said, "Well, then let me help you—I will assist you" and headed toward the bathroom. He began swearing and trying to kick me and was trying to leave the room.

The bathroom is in the classroom. I grabbed his arms and backed him into a corner, like I said, because he was trying to leave the room. He was kicking and scratching on my hand and chest, so I tried to control his legs with my foot. At this point my knee hit him in the groin area, and I let go with one hand because I was afraid that I had hurt M. At this point he used this to his advantage. He bent over in pain, and I thought he was seriously hurt. When he came up, however, he used all his weight . . . and punched me in the right side of my mouth. . . . Another colleague of mine helped me bring him to time-out. . . .

M. became physically out of control and tried to leave the room. Miss T. held him by the arm and prevented him from leaving. This was needed because he was trying to push at her and was becoming a danger to himself as well as others. M. then began trying to kick her. He impacted with her legs several times, causing her to lose her grip on his arm. M. then punched her with a very solid left punch in the face. Miss T. seemed very stunned, and a small amount of blood was visible from the right side of her mouth. She then went to the office, and I brought him to the time-out area.

And that was basically how the incident occurred. I can kind of tell you a little background of the incident. . . . M. had been fighting with another student and was in time-out for a while and was returning from time-out in time to finish lunch. . . . M. was finishing up his lunch, and he was very angry because he was missing out on his computer time because of fighting. That was a guideline that we had set up—that if you were fighting and you miss your lunch, therefore you can't enjoy your specials. And after the incident M. was in time-out for the rest of the day.

In the management of attacks on teachers, as well as other forms of student aggression, it often will prove useful to be aware of other events in the student's life. Such events may help explain (though not excuse) the nature, timing, and severity of the student's behavior. The classroom teacher, school counselor, or other staff member having regular contact with the youth will likely be in the best position to acquire such information. A recent death in the family (Incident 120) and apparent abandonment by the parents (Incident 121) are examples of such significant information.

(120) I was sitting at my desk while my students were completing an assignment. I was grading a paper when I felt something hit me in the eye very hard. I immediately ran out of the room. The student was 12 years old. He had hit me with a ball of clay. The student was a very angry young man. His father had died 3 days before this, and no one had told me or the school. A conference was held with his mother, and we discovered this information. No [disciplinary] action was taken at school. I had a black eye as a result of this incident.

(121) T. was brought to the office for his sexual lewdness. (He had a history of problems in this area and was receiving psychiatric counseling at this time.) He felt he had been unjustly persecuted [and] started "going off" verbally in office with administrators. [He] was admonished to leave the building. We do that frequently. Many of these kids need a cooling down period, and the best thing is to get them out of the building and let them go for a few days. We even do day termination when it's obvious that the child is not connected that day and the day is not going to get any better. We call parents and tell them, "He needs some sleep—he needs to come home." We tell the kids,

"Get your act together, come back tomorrow, we'll talk about it." So that's what we attempted to do with T. And he was refusing to go. [He] literally dug [in] his heels in the hallway and wouldn't leave the building, at which point the principal took his elbow in his hand and was trying to escort him out. . . . T. turned around and started swinging, and he was wrestled to the ground. Because he took a swing at the principal, he was formally suspended and sent to an alternative school. I found out later in the day that on the previous day he had found out that his parents, who had gone to North Carolina to "check it out," had decided that they were not going to come back and get T. to come and live with them.

Incidents 122, 123, and 124 demonstrate that teachers are not the only school personnel who may be attacked by students. Here, respectively, a principal, a vice principal, and a police officer are the victims of such aggression.

(122A—Teacher) During first period on Friday, October 18, Mr. L. came twice to my class looking for a student. The student was not scheduled into my class. A few moments later I heard . . . a verbal confrontation in the hall outside my door. A loud and abusive voice of a female student was heard. I stepped into the hall and observed . . . N. shove Mr. L. with a force that made him lose his balance, and he stumbled across the hall. He then asked her to leave the building. She was argumentative and refused to leave. N. then swung her arm and fist and hit Mr. L. in the face.

(122B—Coteacher) N. ran out of the room, saying, "I'll be back in a minute." Mrs. M. and I both looked at each other in question. I went into the hall and asked N. to come back into the room. She said, "I told that lady (Mrs. M.) I would be back in a minute." I requested again [that she] come in the room. She became loud and very rude, saying, "I don't have to do what you say, and I'll come back when I'm ready." She continued with rude and inappropriate comments. I returned to the room, explained the situation to Mrs. M., and then I walked N. to the office. I explained the situation to Mr. L. The three of us reviewed the problem in his office.

When asked a question by Mr. L., N. was very rude and out of line with her answers. At one point she said, "I don't have to do what you say or anyone else." Mr. L. told her he would sign her out and she would have to return with her mother. I then returned to my room and called Mrs. M. into the hall to inform her of the matter. Mr. L. and N. were also in the hall. N. was looking for someone in the class next door (Mrs. I.). Mrs. M. and I went into our class-room. I then heard a verbal confrontation in the hall. N. was yelling, "I need my cigarettes." Mr. L. demanded she leave the building. As she left she yelled, "Fuck you all."

(123) On October 9, I was in the main office. A call came in from Room 25 for an administrator to come down to remove a student who refused to leave the classroom. Upon entering the classroom, I asked Mr. C., the substitute in charge, who was causing the disturbance. He pointed to a student (U.) who was standing in the front of the room. I asked U. to go to the office repeatedly; she was defiant and refused. She said, "I don't have to go to the office; I want my book." I told her we would get her book for her, but she continued to be defiant and refused to move. At this point I had to physically remove her from the room by grabbing her shoulders. She struggled with me, but I managed to get her into the hallway. I released her and told her to report to the office. She refused in a loud and belligerent voice and said, "I'll go where I want." Then I told her to go to her locker and get her coat because she had the choice of being suspended or cooperating. Again she was defiant. When we reached her locker, she said, "I'm going back to that room now, and you can't stop me." At this point I attempted to prevent her from going back to Room 25 by grabbing her arm. . . . She punched me in the right side of my face near my eye, swearing at me. I told Mr. A., the corridor aide, to get the police officer to escort U. out the door. P. arrived and escorted her out the side door.

(124) On Wednesday, December 2, at approximately 12:55 P.M. Student X and Student Y [were] coming down the hallway in front of the main office. The school police officer was standing in front of a table that sits next to the office

entrance. Student Y [was] fooling around with the police officer when Student X [came] up from behind the officer and [tried] to pull the officer's revolver out of his holster. Although at this point Student X was playing, the officer pushed the student away and asked him never to touch his revolver. Student X is usually a mild-mannered kid, but this time there [were] about 10 to 20 students in the hallway, and Student X, knowing the other students were watching, was not going to let the officer get away with pushing him.

At this point, Student X developed an attitude and told the officer not to put his hands on him again or else. The officer then told the student that he had just better keep his hands to himself. The student walked up closer to the officer, and the officer again extended his arms so that the student couldn't get any closer. The student then pushed the officer, and the officer again extended his arms so that the student couldn't get any closer. The student then pushed the officer's hands down, telling him not to touch him, but by this time the halls were filled with students watching to see what would happen next.

Student X and the officer began pushing one another back and forth, and then the officer started getting angry and grabbed the student by his throat, pressing him up against the wall. Student X [was] steadily fighting to get free. As the officer let go, Student X turned and swung, catching the officer square in the jaw. The officer was caught off guard, probably because the kid was left-handed and he may have been watching the right hand. After the officer had been struck, he fell to the floor, and Student X immediately ran for a side door. The officer jumped up, and, with all the students running and yelling in the hallway, the student wasn't moving very fast, which gave the officer time to catch Student X.

The officer . . . grabbed the student from behind by his throat and was forcing him back into the building. At this point, a teacher on the staff came down along with the vice principal to see what was going on. . . . The teacher, knowing the student very well, reached for the student's left arm and grabbed him by the wrist while creating eye contact so the student would know who was grabbing him. The student looked at the teacher and said, "I'm not going out like that. He had no business putting his hands on me."

Once inside . . . the officer informed the student that he was under arrest and to turn around so he could handcuff him. The student refused and said, "If you come near me I'll hit you again." . . . The secretary called 911 while the teacher and the vice principal restrained the student. . . . At this time the other officers showed up, and the student calmly turned around and was arrested. The student spent approximately 2 weeks in the Public Safety Building and is now out facing charges of assault on a police officer, attempted burglary, and resisting arrest.

The incidents just described portray staff as victims of student aggression. As is the case for student-student fights, they are also a source of potential help. Calls for assistance following an attack on a teacher or other staff member are sometimes answered very swiftly and effectively (Incidents 125 and 126); sometimes, unfortunately, they are not answered at all (Incidents 127 and 128).

(125) My assignment for that particular day was to sub in an urban high school social studies classroom. I've been a long time out of the classroom, probably 4 years or so, and I was real itchy to be with kids and real anxious to teach. I called the classroom teacher and asked him if he would mind if I would do my own lesson rather than just do some kind of busywork sub plan. He said that he had no problem with that, so I went into the class prepared to do basically a workshop on communications. . . . The class went extremely well. . . . And when there were about 20–30 seconds left to the class, we all went to the door, and we were standing there waiting for the bell to ring. And kids were kind of just hanging out, and I was standing right at the entrance, and I saw a teacher that I knew, so we were chatting. . . . I looked, and there were two boys standing chest to chest. . . . The Puerto Rican kid went to punch the black kid in the face, but instead I was in front of the black kid, so he punched me in the face. And I got pushed to the

side, and then all hell broke loose, I mean they were waling on each other. And for a fleeting second I actually tried to intervene again, and then my martial arts training did kick in, and I said, What are you, nuts? So I yelled to the kids— I said, "Get some help" because these two boys were fighting under the office button and I wasn't able to touch the button because they were really going at it right underneath it. Within a short period of time . . . two very large men came in . . . and I heard them say, "OK, at the count of three you take one—I'll take the other." They did break the kids up. . . . How it started is apparently the other kids started this punch-in-the-arm, pass-it-on thing, and each time that it got passed on it got progressively harder until it got to the Puerto Rican kid. He punched the black kid in the arm, and he punched him really hard, and the black kid didn't, in any way, think it was funny. And that was like the beginning of this ruckus. . . . I believe they were both suspended. . . . I went back to the next class. I remember thinking about whether or not I would be able to teach for the rest of the day. . . . I started to think to myself, What if they call the sub for the sub? I said, That's ridiculous. . . . Actually, the pain was all right, and my own calmness kind of returned. So I was able to do that.

(126) At 8:10 A.M., B. raised her hand and asked if she could pass out the DARE folders. I said she could. All other students were seated at their own desks. She passed out the folders. When B. got to X. he questioned her about how she was doing this. She explained and told him to mind his own business. X. said things about B.'s weight, that she [needed] to go on a diet. Through this exchange, I asked them to stop. They ignored me and continued. I raised my voice, asking X. to stop talking and for B. to be seated. B. turned her abusive language toward me. She said I wasn't her mother, couldn't tell her what to do. She shouted this and mumbled profanities under her breath. I said to her to stop talking. She continued shouting at me. I told her that she had to leave because "You do not yell at teachers that way!" She said, "Fuck you, and fuck this shit." I wrote the referral. She refused to leave the room. Then she said she'd take the referral. I handed it to her—she tore

it up. I buzzed the office. Mr. C. was at the room in less than a minute. He asked B. to leave—she refused. He took her arm. She resisted. Mr. C. continued to ask her to leave. She continued to resist. She pushed Mr. C. to the floor. The DARE officer came into the room. Mr. C. and the DARE officer forcibly escorted B. from the room. The office called and asked X. to come down a few minutes later.

(127) During the last period of the day, March 12, I was attacked by a student in my class. I had requested aid from the office . . . on four occasions during that hour. The office was busy, and no one could come to remove the student. About 10 minutes before the end of the class period, the student got up out of his seat, and when I asked him to sit back down and pulled his chair out so he could sit back down, the student punched me in the face. I put out my hand and held on to his shirt to hold him off, and he twisted away from me and in the process knocked me down. As a consequence my foot was broken. I had my son and daughter in my room at the time, so they helped me to my car and took me to the doctor. I was unable to get a sub for the next day, so I went into class on crutches. During my conference period that day, my father took me to the County Sheriff's Department substation to file a complaint. They refused to take my complaint and referred me to the courthouse. . . . They could not take my complaint because [the student] was a minor and told me to go to the courthouse in Q. We went there, and again no one would take the complaint. We were then referred to the Youth Court Lockup in Q. There someone took my complaint. . . . No action was taken on my complaint. . . . As of this date, almost a year later, no further action has taken place. The student was expelled from our school district for the remainder of that school year.

(128) I was 6 months pregnant and preparing to enter into my second-floor typing class. One particularly hyperaggressive boy refused to come into the classroom from the balcony walkway. I went from the doorway of the classroom to the student, who was standing by the rail, to ask him again to come to class. He refused again, got angry

with me, and tried to push me over the rail onto the courtyard below. I freaked—yelled for the teacher in the next class to come to my room while I went to the office. The teacher came to watch my room. I went to the principal quite shaken and tried to explain to him what had happened. He accused me of being nonprofessional for leaving my room, wrote up a reprimand to put in my personnel file, and nothing was ever done to the student.

Teachers have every right to be safe from attacks, to have the opportunity to learn effective means to deal with student attacks, and to expect swift and competent assistance from others in the school when an attack does occur. What teachers do not have a right to do is to counterattack—to hit a student in return for being hit. As understandable and as reflexive as such responses are, they are not appropriate teacher behaviors. The teacher in Incident 129 who physically strikes the student who had punched him is, no less than the student, engaging in assaultive behavior. Similarly unequivocally inappropriate teacher responses are cursing at a student (Incident 130), spitting at a student (Incident 131), washing out a student's mouth with soap (Incident 132), and pushing a student into a puddle of his own urine (Incident 133)!

(129) There was a student . . . getting very aggressive and . . . meaning to hurt another student. The student who wanted to fight was removed from class by myself. I told him that I was taking him to time-out. He got more aggressive, and he punched me "right where it counts." As a natural human reflex, my fist clenched, and I hit him very, very hard in the ribs. From that day on this student has not raised a fist to any staff member. I don't believe in inflicting physical pain on a student, but that seemed to work.

(130) A situation would be where kids know me outside of my work environment, where they're familiar with my family or familiar with my younger sisters and they're familiar with these people, and so it's very easy for them to make comments or to say things. Even though you're supposed to be the adult and you're supposed to be professional, they do get to you. And I found that some students can make a comment like "Oh, yeah, I know your sister, and she's . . . a little

hooker." . . . I think the best thing to do is remain professional—don't let it get personal. . . . I've allowed that to get to me, and I've made comments about people's mothers, and their mothers' and grandparents' body parts, and things like that. . . . I had a student who was supposed to be working, decided he wasn't going to work, and was sent back to the desk. And the comments [were] made to me "Oh, you whorish bitch, just go fuck yourself. . . . Your mom's a whore. . . . Fuck you, and your sister, and your mother, and . . . I hope your dead folks die." . . . I found myself in an exchange of words with that student—I mean not as a teacher to student but as . . . person to person. And I'm an adult here, and I was exchanging words with an 11-year-old and talking about his mother and his aunt. I really had to catch myself because I knew I was wrong. . . . I had to leave the classroom, come back in. . . . As soon as you're aggressive with a student . . . they're not going to respect you. You're not the teacher. You're not the adult in the room. . . . You could be a student as far as they're concerned—you're on that level.

(131) I've had a student who had to be restrained in time-out. I put him in time-out: "OK, I'm going to behave." I let him up, and he did begin spitting and spit all over me. . . . I took off his socks . . . and I began to wipe up. He had spit on the walls and window, and I took his clothing and I began to wipe up where he spit. . . . I tossed his clothes back, and it wasn't anything to be spiteful. . . . I've seen [another teacher] whose students have taken other students' clothes and spit on them or spit at other students, and she went right up, and she took [a student's] coat and spit on it and [said], "Now how do you feel?"

(132) One day I was walking through the cafeteria and O. and all his friends started laughing and pointing at me. Then one of the boys approached me and said, "Ms. C., O.'s over there disrespecting you. Do you want me to take care of him?" I responded by saying, "Thanks for the backup, but let's just ignore O., OK?" The student then said, "But Ms. C., he's telling all the boys that you're going to suck his, ya know, dick!" At this point O. approached me and said,

"Yeah, I told them you're going to suck my dick. So what?"
Well, I had enough of this kid's abuse since calls home and
to his parole officer, as well as going to the principal's office,
all failed to help modify O.'s behavior. I took matters into
my own hands. I had a great rapport with the other "gang
members," so I felt secure saying, "You're right, I'll suck it
now! I got my knee pads on." Well, this boy was shocked,
embarrassed. His friends started chanting, "Go O., go O.,
go O." I again said, "Let's go. Do you want it or not?" He then
replied, "Man! Leave me alone," and boy was he embarrassed.

Then I said, "Well, perhaps you'd rather go to the office"
and off we went. When we got to the office I realized he
would receive no consequence, so I said, "OK, O., we can
wait here for an administrator, or you can get some soap in
your foul mouth." O. said, "I'll take the soap." He chose the
brand and the amount, and he even opened his mouth.
When I proceeded to squirt the soap in his mouth, he
jumped up and said, "You crazy! I'm not messing around
with you anymore." O. and I got along fine after this.

(133) The incident that I'm describing all happened at one
time. This all took place as a sequence of events. And so like
I said, he exposed himself. "Kiss my ass" I think [was] his
choice of words, and suck this and suck that. And he actually
urinated on the floor. And before he did it, he actually
announced he was going to do it. He was going to piss on
the floor (of the time-out room). And I told him, because
he had done this before and there was really, I don't want
to say there was no punishment for it because he did have
to clean it up, but just cleaning it up didn't seem to be
effective enough to prevent him from doing it again, or else
he wouldn't have threatened to do it again. So, you know
he says, "I'm going to piss on the floor." I said, "OK, you
do it, and you're going to end up in it," and I was dead
serious. And I don't know if he just didn't care that I was
serious or not or if he just didn't think I'd do it. . . . Anyway,
he urinated on the floor, and I did put him down in it,
which caused an entire mess. . . . It was a big mess as far as
parents and administration. I was reprimanded for my
actions. And even though I was reprimanded I don't think

I was wrong because he really deserved it. . . . If it was my choice and if he did it again, he'd get the same consequences, and he hasn't urinated on the floor since. . . . I don't think being aggressive towards a student who is being aggressive is effective either, but you have to let them know there are serious consequences for your actions. And like I said, if they go to an extreme, you have to go to an extreme sometimes.

Group Aggression

In addition to out-of-control behavior, student-student fights, and student attacks on teachers or other school personnel, another form of high-level student aggression is perpetrated in groups. Such incidents are even more dangerous, more difficult to control, and more likely to result in bodily harm. In its least virulent expression, group aggression appears as collective threat (Incident 134) or collective bullying (Incident 135). Both of these incidents were handled quite well, the first by a school safety officer, who detained the youth more or less leading the threatening group so that those being threatened could depart. In the second incident, the teacher employed a group incentive system to successfully eliminate the collective bullying behavior.

> (134) On March 27 at approximately 2:15 P.M., after the majority of the students had left school, there was a group of students (approximately 10–12) who were standing around and not leaving. I walked over to the group of students and told them all to leave, that school was over. There were three or four boys standing together who did not leave. . . . From the looks of these boys, who looked scared or just intimidated, I got the idea that there was some type of problem, possibly a fight brewing, and that this group of boys did not want any part of it and were waiting for the other half to leave, thus attempting to avoid any conflict. I asked the boys who was giving them trouble, and one pointed to a student whom I know as C. I asked them if it was C., and one shook his head yes, but I could tell by their actions that they were intimidated or scared and did not want to make it known that they were. I know C. and that he tries to be a tough guy. . . . I have had personal dealings with C. in that he is unruly and mouthy. I specifically told C. to leave and also told the three or four others who appeared to be hanging with C. to leave. C. then turned

toward me and began to tell me that I was a shithead, asshole, smelly cop and what was I going to do. I started walking toward C., continuing to tell him to leave, and he kept up the verbal abuse, while walking backwards making sure to keep a distance of approximately 20 feet between me and him. At this point, it was par for the course for C., and at least he was walking away from the school as I initially requested of him. But then it turned into a big game for C. Not only did he continue the verbal abuse, but now he was circling around and walking back toward school. Now I realized he was not going to leave, thus allowing these other boys to go home without fear. I told C. I [had] had enough, that he was to go to the office now. C. questioned that and continued to run away from me, dancing all around, playing his game. I was able to grab C. by his arm and direct him to the school office. C. continued his typical show as other students were watching. I sat C. in the office for about 30 minutes before allowing him to leave in order to give the other boys enough time to leave school without any trouble.

(135) I had a target kid in my room, and the other students were constantly hitting him. So we decided to keep a chart for the month, and if they didn't hit him we'd go bowling. The hitting reduced dramatically, and we went bowling. After bowling . . . we started the check sheet for the next month. Again they avoided hitting him, and we went bowling. From this point on we had very little hitting and once a month did something special.

More difficult to manage than the foregoing incidents, and certainly more dangerous, are incidents in which several fights occur simultaneously (Incidents 136 and 137). These situations can lead to serious injury to student and teacher alike (Incident 138). Each of these incidents offers lessons of value for the effective resolution of collective student aggression. In Incident 136, the animosities long existing between two groups in the community were played out in the school. Schools are indeed part of the community in which they are located, and thus awareness of events in the community can help predict school violence. A good informal intelligence system, an anonymous hot line, good teacher-student and teacher-parent relationships, and a visible and available school administration may help contribute to awareness that trouble is brewing and increase the likelihood of heading it off. Incident 137 highlights the prevention-focused need for extra security at public events and value of an "all-come code" arrangement for the speedy summoning of assistance to a fight scene. Incident 138 offers two useful messages. The first concerns the likely value of formal restraint and containment training, which, in this case, might have reduced the chances of a teacher's nose being broken. The second concerns a reluctant security guard, who provided no security and did not guard. As for previously described failures to provide assistance, this failure to respond ought itself to be severely consequated.

> (136) Actually, it was an incident out in the community that had been occurring over probably a couple of years between one large family of 25 and the other kids in the community and the supporters of the other kid. . . . Six of the kids go to the high school, and then there are several cousins that go, so they consist of a large group. And one of the young ladies was having a problem with another young lady in the community. And it was the type of thing that would carry over into the school and just get bigger and bigger, and more kids wanted to get involved and side up with each other. . . . Just a lot of back and forth talk and a lot of kids just trying to get something going between the two young ladies.
>
> It boiled up . . . and the young ladies were sharing the same lunch hour, and there was always this show of power. I mean, when they went outside of the cafeteria into the courtyard, one young lady would have maybe five members, and then they would look at the other group and there would be three or four there. . . . They were just kind of positioning themselves for a show of power. . . . It led to the two young ladies with their supporters behind them, going face-to-face. . . . It didn't escalate so much there, but what happened was a number of kids started saying that something was happening. Then you have a rush of kids. . . . Some kids were rushing from all over to this scene, and eventually a fight did break out in the hallway as some of the young ladies from both sides were being taken to the principal's

office. One of the girls broke away and actually attacked the young lady from the other side, and a fight broke out between three or four students then. And security was finally able to break it up. They even had to handcuff some of the girls to chairs to keep them in the office, trying to calm things down. In the meantime, a call was sent out for the police. . . . And it was just kind of . . . a frenzy, so they needed some police officers to remove kids from the campus who were not leaving voluntarily upon request. . . . There were a total of 17 students involved. We have a progressive disciplinary policy that we use, so there were suspensions for involvement from 3 to 10 days. And then there were students involved in actually attacking the security. Those students went before the Board of Education with the recommendation for expulsion.

(137) In this case what we had was seven girls involved, and to make it even more difficult four of them were North students, one of them was a student at another school, [and] one of them is no longer a student. . . . She had graduated from another school, and the seventh was at an alternative school. . . . Parents of all of these people were notified, and all of [the students] were arrested or at least taken into custody and taken to the police station. And the reason for that was that this seven-person fight presented what we felt was just about the worst scenario we had envisioned. All fights are dangerous to participants, but this fight had occurred around 9:30 or 10:00 in the evening after a talent show that was put on every year. . . . At that talent show the kids are there, their parents, grandparents, aunts, uncles, little brothers and sisters, and in some cases infants. So what had happened is that the talent show itself went smoothly. Everybody was leaving. The concourse area adjoining our gymnasium, where the event was held, was simply packed with people who were leaving the facility, and at that point, as near as we can track down, a couple of girls said something as a couple of other girls passed. Now who said what we never could nail down because there were conflicting versions of "she said this" . . . but obviously somebody said something. . . . Originally, I think it was two girls fighting, and immediately their friends joined in. So we had four girls on one side, three on another. It was a fight that was

bad in another way. Not only was it dangerous to all these innocent people—grandparents and little kids who were attending and who happened to be in the area—but it was near glass walls that students there could possibly have been thrown against, glass display cases. Clothes were literally ripped off the girls. . . .

We're talking about hitting, punching, biting, tearing, ripping, everything. It was a fight that was dangerous in the sense that we could not at first get it stopped. As fast as we could grab two girls here, the other two would start, and then as we grabbed them somebody else would jump in. . . . We had a combination of teachers, administrators, and our own internal security who were grabbing kids and at one point literally picking people up and carrying them up to various offices, at which point we ran out of offices. . . . Adults were stationed with them to make sure they couldn't get away. . . .

But our immediate response is . . . get the people out of the crowd that are participating, get them somewhere else, and break the crowd up that's observing. . . . Then everybody grabbed notebooks and paper and everything and started interviewing immediately. . . . Once we knew what direction that was going we called C. area police and asked them to respond. Because it had become so ugly we literally felt like at that point these people needed to be taken into custody. That sends a message to them, it helps us by restoring order, at least as far as those kids, and of course it sends a message to the parents and the whole community that we don't tolerate that, and so the police did respond. . . . We convinced them to . . . at least take the students to the police station and force their parents to come up there to pick them up.

(138) I was sitting in the guidance office at a large high school in the downtown area, and this high school is noted for a tremendous amount of violence, a tremendous amount of fighting and unrest among the student body. I saw 100 or so students go running to class. . . . So I went outside pretty quickly, and it looked to be about 200 to 300 students milling around. Several fights had broken out. I could see an administrator, who was of short stature and who had been pressed into teaching service after having not taught

for 20 years or so, standing out there saying, "Gentlemen, gentlemen." He was being totally ignored, and kids were stabbing each other with hairpicks right around him. So I went over and took the kid away who was trying to stab the other one behind the ear, and I moved him away from the fight area, and actually in a fairly gentle way had my arm on him and brought him with me. I had to leave about 100 feet, and I'm moving away from this large crowd with about 300 students. As I'm moving down I see a security guard who's at a gate. I motioned to him to come and help. He pulled one of these slow-motion movements towards me, hoping that I had the whole thing done before he ever got there. It was obvious. He doesn't want to get involved. So I'm walking down with the student who is involved in this fight, and out of the crowd comes a slim student who comes up to me with sort of a smile on his face. He comes up, not running, but advancing towards me—a total sucker punch. I didn't expect him to do anything. He came up to me and punches me quickly in the nose—broke my nose. I started bleeding profusely. . . . The security guard finally arrives on the scene much, much too late, and the guard proceeds to handcuff him. The guard is small. He takes out his billy club, and he's about to beat him over the head, at which point I help subdue the kid and get handcuffs put on him. At this point I'm bleeding like a pig. . . . The nose was badly broken, so they took me to the hospital. . . . The student was expelled . . . and removed from the school district.

Incident 139 is different from the others in this section, one of the most serious instances of student aggression in this book. Rather than groups of students fighting with one another, here a group of students attack and beat a teacher. Several observations emerge from this incident, all of which relate to the fight management recommendations presented earlier (see Table 2):

- Do hit the call button or send a student for help first.
- Never place yourself between two (or more) fighting students.
- Let the students fight unless you are trained as a skilled fight intervenor.

- Send away, seek to control, or at least be aware of the audience of students observing the fight.

- If injured, tend to your own physical and emotional needs. (This teacher, as is so common for those in this circumstance, returned to work the next day!)

(139) I turned from the blackboard, and I saw the two students were facing each other. The female teacher was between them, and she was facing the male student. And she was yelling in no uncertain terms for him, calling him by his first name and telling him to stop. Meanwhile, behind her, I could see that the female student was trying to punch the male student by going around the female teacher. . . . I thought I would . . . approach the female student from the rear. . . . I wanted to make sure she knew who I was and that I was a teacher. And so I didn't want to just sneak up behind her and grab her. . . . So when I came in . . . I reached across, and I grabbed her left wrist. . . . I identified myself and said, "This is Mr. B.—the fight is over." I called her by her first name. . . . She continued on around and began striking me in the side of my face with her right hand, with her fist clenched. I then immediately let go of her wrist and put my arms around her, trying to pin her arms at her side. . . . She started struggling. And I think I wasn't really ready for the struggle because she more or less pulled me toward the back of the room. . . . She then tripped over the corner of a desk, and she fell flat on her back with me landing up on top of her. . . . I saw another student. . . . He was the original student who was involved with the altercation (the male student). I saw him coming at me from the other side of the room, and it was obvious from his movement that he was going to try to kick me. . . . As he swung his leg around, I immediately jerked my head back. . . . It was only a very minor glancing blow in the area of my left temple. OK, the next thing that almost immediately happened from my side was someone had kicked me in the right ribs and someone had kicked me in the left side. . . . It was another male student. . . . I immediately pushed off the floor as quickly as possible. . . . Most of the students around me then ran from the room. . . . I immediately went over to

what we call . . . the "panic button" to call the main office.
. . . I told them that we need principals and we need security.
. . . Within . . . 2 or 3 minutes security and the principal
showed up. I explained to them what had happened. . . .
Security left the area to try and find the students involved.
I then informed the assistant principal . . . that I was
assaulted for no apparent reason other than I was trying
to break up this fight and that I would like to press charges
against the students involved and charge them with assault.
And I would ask that he would call the G. police. . . . I also
complained to him [that] my ribs were bothering me. . . .
The next thing I was taken by one of the security persons
to the first aid station out in G., where I was X-rayed and
examined. . . . This pain continued on for like 2 or 3 months
when I would take a breath or pressure or something like
that. . . . Sometime later I got information from the school
district that they had suspended the students for 10 days
with a recommendation that it would be a 90-day suspension,
and they also recommended that they be expelled from
school. . . .

I went back to work the next morning, even though I was
suffering quite a bit of pain. . . . I just felt that it was best
that I be there. . . .

Later on in the year . . . I went to . . . two board hearings.
And the two male students, the one that had kicked me in
the head and the one I identified that kicked me in the ribs,
were expelled. The female student . . . was also expelled.

Group aggression by students in America's schools has in recent
years taken an especially ominous form—gang violence. There are
approximately 200,000 members of juvenile gangs in the United
States, and a majority of these youths are of school age.[5] This collective
phenomenon, as much as anything else, has helped end the era in
which the school setting has been "neutral turf." Gangs have indeed
come to school, as Incidents 140, 141, and 142 starkly depict. Yet
with sufficient prior planning, personnel, and attention to effective
fight management tactics, gang violence can be contained and
reduced. Incident 143 illustrates a good start in this direction. Here
an adequate number of skilled school personnel intervene swiftly,

isolate and interview the disputants, compare versions, institute prescriptive consequences (i.e., different consequences for different youths depending on past aggression history and current involvement), and reach out to parents.

(140) The "Bloods" and the "Crips" had been fanning a fire between the two for weeks. There had been a fight several weeks before between the two gang members. . . . The whole school was up in arms over it. One day "all hell broke loose." Students preplanned to come to school armed to the hilt. A schoolwide fight ensued. Blood was flowing profusely. The police were called in. Several students were cut. The cops finally succeeded in breaking it all up. The kids were suspended for 15 days.

(141) On April 27, K. assaulted student D. The fight occurred during first period and seemed to be premeditated. The school administrators believe the fight was gang related. Police were called, and K. was taken into custody. Later he was released by the police and shot while walking down the road in a drive-by shooting. When the fight occurred, K. was dressed in a red shirt, a red hat, and had on a red bandanna.

(142) The incident I'm going to talk about is a major fight in the cafeteria . . . which involved about 11 kids. I think 9 . . . of them got kicked out of school for the rest of the year. It was gang related. Most of our problems start in the neighborhood and then end up at school. . . . This fight involved kids in the cafeteria . . . throwing chairs at each other, punching each other. There was blood everywhere, tables tipped over. . . . I was the only one in the cafeteria on duty. All the other teachers at the table ran into the kitchen and locked the door and hid. . . . I tackled two or three different kids and cracked my kneecap trying to break it up, and I finally got things separated. And there was literally 9 to 11 kids involved, and they kicked them out, the majority of them, for the rest of the year. . . . That probably is the most major disruption that I've had here in 22 years. . . . I guess kids really do believe that, out in the neighborhood especially, they need to wear colors and be affiliated with somebody for protection, and then it ends up at school, too. . . .

The parties were separated into different offices. The parents came. I'm not sure if the police were involved—I think they were.

(143) This incident focused on the actions of three or four young men at our school, basically 9th and 10th graders. . . . The initial reason for the investigation was a fight between two students. And we assumed it was a typical one-on-one, I-don't-like-you, you-bumped-into-me kind of a fight, which occurs on a fairly regular basis. . . . We found out very quickly that this was not just a one-on-one spontaneous fight, but that this particular fight related to two rival gangs in the neighborhood in our school. The two gangs, one's called the "Downtowners" and one's called "Fifteenth Street Boys." The participants in both of those groups were 15- to 17-year-old males, mostly white. And what we found out is that the members of both groups had been for a time in conflict because one group was more established and one group was an up-and-coming group. And the up-and-coming group had decided that they were going to take over the action. . . . It came down to just a feeling of turf and who's in charge. So this particular fight, in questioning the students involved, we began with the two students that I had observed out the back window of the school fighting. . . . We, when I say we—me and a couple of other administrators—brought them into separate offices, which is our usual procedure. We will isolate the participants, interview them independently, take down the names . . . their version of what happened, and then compare versions between the two students. . . . The two fighters were kind of the designated leaders of each group, and so they were representing their groups. . . . Just prior to the incident that I saw there had been several members of both groups that also fought or were starting to fight. . . . It ended up with four students being suspended, after the investigation, for 10 days and then requests made for an extension due to the district policy about gang-related violence. So once we established, in the interviews, that really this was not just a one-on-one spontaneous fight but related [to] gang rivalries, we used the discipline code to get extended suspensions for the two main participants and short suspensions for a couple of the hangers-on that had

really been engaged in just kind of a scuffle. . . . We did interview witnesses. We took notes, compared versions. . . . We then notified the parents by phone, sent follow-up letters indicating specifically what happened, and then had a district-level disciplinary meeting that extended the 10-day suspension.

Exemplars

The aggression management lessons we have offered have been many and varied as we have considered low-, mid-, and high-level forms of such student behavior. Both "do's" and "don'ts" have been suggested. The present section attempts to pull together and integrate these suggestions by presenting a small series of "exemplar incidents." These are success stories, incidents at each of the three levels of student aggression in which school personnel choose and use combinations of interventions to effectively reduce or eliminate the problematic behavior. For each incident described, we indicate the intervention procedures successfully employed.

> (144) Class is writing paragraphs about the activity they did the day before. Noise level in class is rising gradually. Before it gets too noisy so she can't be heard, teacher says, "Freeze," then repeats herself. Most of the kids stop right away what they are doing. She says, "Remember, *freeze* means stop right where you are whatever you are doing and listen." Then teacher says, "This is writing time, which is quiet time. It is not quiet in here, and I need it to be quiet so I can think and so others can think about what they are writing. Now go back to writing." Noise level in class drops again and then rises again. This time she raises her hand in the air and as students see her hand up they raise theirs, and if they were out of their seats they move to their own seats. She starts counting down, five to one, and at one notes which tables are quiet and working and gives them a star on the chart.

Intervention procedures

- Rule reminder
- Rule explanation
- Reward for appropriate behavior

(145) Student horsing around in classroom, poking other students. Teacher quietly catches her eye and motions for her to go to time-out desk. This child has been disruptive on and off all morning and has been warned. Teacher leaves her in time-out while rest of class is working on a project. After about 10 minutes, student is clearly getting angry because she hasn't been allowed to return to group. Calls out to teacher. Teacher ignores. Student kicks over a chair. Teacher ignores. Student finally settles down and sits there looking like she's ready to kill, but is quiet. Teacher then goes over to her and allows her to go back to group.

Intervention procedures

- Time-out
- Extinction

(146) Teacher is waiting to begin math assignment. Class is having hard time getting settled down. First she asks, quietly, for them to stop doing any other work they are doing. Then she raises her hand in the air. Students around the room begin to raise their hands in the air. There are still a few pockets of disturbance. Teacher starts counting down from five. Five, four, three, two, one. Says, "Table 1 is ready—they get a star. Table 4 is ready—they get a star. Table 5 is ready—they get a star. Tables 2 and 3 are almost ready. Table 6 needs to get ready." She walks over to chart on board and puts a star on the chart for Tables 1, 4, and 5. All six tables are listed, with varying numbers of stars after the table number. . . . Reward system is based on number of stars: Twenty stars means 20 minutes of free time. As she gives stars she says to tables getting stars, "I like the way everyone at Tables 1, 4, and 5 all have their pencils and paper out on the table and are sitting quietly ready to work. This is great."

Intervention procedures

- Rule reminder
- Warning
- Catch them being good
- Praise and privilege rewards

(147) Two large, athletic half-adolescent boys [were] in a group playing basketball. . . . One became very agitated. An argument ensued, resulting in the larger of the boys (referred to as A.) kicking the lower part of the leg of the other boy (referred to as B.), knocking him to the floor. As B. began to stand up to fight, A. became increasingly hostile. At that moment I intervened, using deescalating assertiveness techniques called "broken record" and positive assertion.

I moved to the location of the two boys, calmly asking the other children in close proximity to help me out by staying back from those two boys. . . . I positioned myself about 3 feet from them between and to the side.

I briefly stated to B., "Stay!" while holding out my hand indicating "Stop!" A.'s behavior was escalating. I repeated his name monotonously, over and over, until I got his attention (broken record), then asserted, "Don't get yourself in trouble!"

I repeated this process three times, making brief statements like "Just go outside."

When he finally did, I went out to him. I asked him to stay and said I would come back in 10–15 minutes to see how he was. I called back up to [the office for someone to] handle the gym, then counseled.

Intervention procedures

- Urging audience away
- Calm, defusing talk
- Firm directives
- "Broken record" instructions
- Counseling

(148) Two students began exchanging verbal "shots" at each other toward the end of a class period. When reminded that this was inappropriate, they ceased their verbal exchange; however, both were still visibly angry. The class period ended very shortly after this, and all of the students began to leave the room and go outside. Once outside, the two students began to get in each other's face, escalated

their verbal exchange, and one began to shove the other. I walked up at this point and stood close to the students and quietly, but firmly, told each student to go sit at a picnic table (the tables were on opposite sides of a sidewalk). Once they were separated, I sent a student to get another teacher to take the class to a classroom so they were not standing around watching. Once the area was cleared, I went to each table and listened to their account of what happened. I tried to explain that I understood their frustration in being called a name; however, the action that they took (being physically aggressive) was not appropriate. We discussed alternative reactions and role-played these once they had calmed down more. Each student was asked to write their account of what had happened before they forgot the details, and consequences for fighting were given to them.

Intervention procedures

- Rule reminder
- Calm, defusing talk
- Separating protagonists
- Removing audience
- Interviewing separately
- Setting limits
- Practicing alternatives

(149) It was midway through the afternoon (Friday), and I was with a master teacher and her seventh-grade class in the library. . . . From over my shoulder I heard an escalating exchange of increasingly menacing threats between a male in the library and one in the hallway just outside of the library entrance. . . . Caustic comments changed to challenging threats, and at that point (only about 5–8 seconds had elapsed) I headed quickly for where the two boys were. . . .

Although the boy I did not know appeared the aggressor, I faced the boy from the class I was responsible for and stepped in front of him, directing him in a soft, low, but firm voice to walk away. . . .

I have broken up many fights, and the golden rule for me is to only address one of the individuals involved—never try to arbitrate at the stage that they are about to fight. Use words (clear and directive), but keep them brief, soft but firm, and don't ask any questions, for this tends to just escalate the bad feelings and provide fuel for accusations. Instead, tell the individual whom you have chosen to move away and comment on the time ("Not now . . ."). I also say the words almost rhythmically. I believe that the way messages are conveyed can soothe and ameliorate a person's mood. . . .

Be cautious to put one's body in the way of the individual being confronted, but . . . keep the other person in your peripheral vision. You want to let the other person know that you can see him but that your attention is elsewhere. This helps put the other person in the role of spectator rather than performer. . . .

After being polite and offering the individual that you have confronted about 3 seconds in which to save face and walk away, you need to quickly begin to move the person you have confronted away from the other. . . . Position your body so that as the person walks away from you, he is headed also away from the other boy. Then you may contend with the remaining person. . . . Repeat your firm entreaty/directive to "Move away so you can cool yourself down."

In this incident the boy did not heed my directives, so I put my palms gently but firmly on his upper arms and began moving backwards while I rhythmically commanded him to "Just walk away—you don't need this." . . . He let the other boy know by slightly resisting me that he was not afraid, but he did back up as I pressured him steadily. As he gave in a bit and continued backing up I allowed for a bit more space (from less than 1 foot to about 2 feet) between us and looked over my shoulder, where I saw that the vice principal had "taken down" the other boy. . . .

I heard from a teacher that the boy taken away in handcuffs had a history of very violent episodes in the school and so was handled more severely than the boy I contended with.

Intervention procedures

- Calm, defusing talk
- Safe interposing
- Awareness of audience
- Helping disputants save face
- Firm directives

(150) I had a class of eighth graders (25 students) a couple of years ago whom I called my "class from hell." It was a seventh-period class (the last class of the day), and they came to me straight from lunch. It was clear from the moment they walked into the classroom on the first day that they intended to run the class, and they were horrible most of the time. They talked constantly, refused to work, and generally had no respect for themselves, each other, or me. The only way I knew I could handle them was to make my classroom rules very clear, make the consequences of infractions very clear, and then be diligent in applying those consequences. One of my major consequences, besides after-school detentions, was a phone call home to parents (all of whom I'd already had "get acquainted" phone or in-person conferences with), and I was on the phone with parents from this class every night. I also had had parent conferences with most of the parents by the second marking period because of behavior problems. Interestingly enough, all the parents I contacted were extremely supportive. They were having the same kinds of problems with these kids at home that I was having in the classroom. . . .

I'm stating all this so that you will understand the context in which the incident I am about to relate took place. It was, I think, late November when this took place (after the Thomas nomination to the Supreme Court [and] Anita Hill [testimony] on sexual harassment). There was one young woman whom I had had a lot of trouble with at the very beginning of the school year. . . . She was a very pretty girl, and over the past year had gone from being physically a very young 12-year-old to a fully mature 13-year-old. . . . She also had been very much of a tomboy and an athlete (she still played on the girls' basketball team) and related to the boys very much as a chum. However, even if she wasn't always aware of the change in their relationship . . . the boys sure were. I had been aware of this sexual tension, but it's something that as a middle school teacher you are always aware of, and after a while you come to accept as the norm in a middle school environment. But in late November I began to be aware that there was more than the usual tension in the air, and I began to watch more closely for what was causing it.

Again, as is typical in a middle school, the physical development of the girls was far ahead of the boys, but because of retentions, I had a number of eighth-grade boys in that class who were 15+ years old. And these 15-year-olds were not only very aware of H.'s development, but they had begun to make very quiet comments to her. . . . It all came to a head one day when one of the boys became more brazen than he had been in the past. That day she had on a very pretty peasant blouse and jeans, but the blouse was cut low enough in the front that her ample cleavage was clearly visible. What he said to her was why didn't she lean over so he could see more. . . . Seven or eight of the other boys in the class immediately formed a circle around H. and got on the bandwagon of "Yeah, lean over." . . . H. at that point was in tears. I blew up, told the boys and the rest of the class to get started on the day's work (which I always posted on the front blackboard), and took H. out into the hall. There we talked about exactly what had happened, what had been said, and how long this had been going on. . . . At first H. had been complimented that he was noticing her. Then I think she became embarrassed but didn't know what to do about it. I came back in the room, wrote a referral on the boy who had initiated the comment, and told the other boys that I would be calling their parents that night to talk about what had happened. I said to them, "What you did was sexual harassment, and you could be in big trouble for it." I told them that I expected to never hear anything like that from them again.

After school that day I went down to my principal's office and told her what had happened, what I wanted done with the kid on referral (in-school suspension plus some counseling with the school psychologist). I wanted a big impression made on this kid. . . . My principal was totally supportive. . . . I then went to the counselor in the building that H. had established a relationship with and talked with her about what happened. . . .

The boy whom I sent the referral on was given in-school suspension by the administration, and I called his parents and the parents of the other boys that night. . . .

I had expected to hear from at least one of the parents, "Oh, well, boys will be boys. It really isn't that serious." But I really think that the Anita Hill, Clarence Thomas hearings had so sensitized the community to sexual harassment . . . that I didn't get anything but support from them. . . . All of the parents agreed that this was a serious matter and that they would talk to their boys about it.

The last interesting piece of all of this was the reaction and attitudes of the other girls in the class. There was a change in the way they reacted to me. They were less defiant, more cooperative, and generally didn't give me as hard a time. I don't mean they were angels. But there was a subtle shift for the better in their behavior.

Intervention procedures

- Positive parent conferences early in term
- Interviewing victim
- Referral
- Informing administrators and counselor
- Calls to parents
- In-school suspension

(151) Well, this incident was kind of a straightforward . . . easy fight to deal with . . . and to reconcile the opposing forces. What I had was two students, 10th-grade male students brought to me by one of the cafeteria supervisors, and there had been a fight. . . . What had happened was at

lunch there were about a half-dozen freshman, sophomore boys . . . and one of them had thrown lettuce at another student, and of course that student reciprocated by throwing part of his sandwich back. Pretty soon they were throwing real heavy food, at which point several other boys kind of egged them on. . . . One of the guys realized he was now in a position where he couldn't really back down, and he'd run out of food, so he said something about "Let's handle this now." The other kid said, "OK, just follow me down here," and they walked down to the opposite end very close by and hit each other about two to three times. It was broken up immediately by other students and one of the cafeteria supervisors, who brought them to my office. Well, the investigation was very straightforward. Again, we did isolate them in separate offices. One of the other principals interviewed one, and I interviewed one—we got almost virtually the same identical story: [He] threw food at me, and I threw it back, and he threw more, and I threw more, and then we got mad and hit each other. So we compared those two versions again, and both students had really clean records. . . . Another thing we always look at is have there been previous fights. So for these guys, not only was this their first fight, but it was also virtually their first discipline referral of any kind. So there was no doubt in my mind after we checked through this and talked also with a couple of witnesses that this would be the minimum we'd go on a fight (which is 3 days according to policy). I called both boys' parents. . . . Both boys agreed it was a stupid fight—it never should have happened. Both apologized, did all the right things right down the line, and it was very clear they really did honestly regret the whole incident, and that's probably the key factor as far as many of the things we looked at, including what caused the fight, was it premeditated, was it spontaneous, could either of the individuals have avoided it. (Well, obviously they could have avoided it, but it happened so quickly, being adolescents they just didn't think through it real clearly.) Also, with their previous record all the policy calls for is suspension. It didn't have to be over 3 days, and I told that to the parents and then sent the follow-up letter indicating the reasons for the suspension and that they could come back: Just simply have them both report to my office on the day they were due to return, check with them to make sure nothing had happened to make the conflict flare up. Sometimes that happens when we send them home—everything seems to be OK, and they get back to school, and there's been another problem. Everything was cool, so after 3 days they came back to school.

Intervention procedures

- Isolating disputants

- Interviewing disputants separately

- Interviewing witnesses

- Calls to parents

- Reciprocal apologies

- Suspension

- Checking situation before suspension ends

(152) In a junior high classroom of 30 students, two students began interacting with each other in a picking-on manner ("Faggot" and "Yo mama"), which quickly escalated into loud accusations and blows by both students.

By the time the teacher crossed the room to the students, both were fully involved in hitting each other and hurting each other. A child was sent to the office for help (no alarm is available to communicate to the office). The next-door teacher came over to assist.

Some students just sat still, some were yelling, taking sides verbally, more helped the teacher get them apart.

The teacher pulled back on one while stating loudly and firmly to stop. The students continued to lunge at each other. By that time the other teacher was able to restrain the other student. Later, the principal came, talked to them, recorded both students' and teachers' statements, and called the parents in for a conference. Put both immediately into on-campus, remote, in-school suspension for a 3-day period of time. . . .

The students met with the school counselor daily for talk-it-out time and discussed alternatives for student choice.

Intervention procedures

- Calling for help
- Waiting for help before restraining students
- Firm directives
- Interviewing disputants
- Parent conference
- In-school suspension
- Counseling

Special Topics

We wish to present and examine three remaining types of aggression-relevant incidents. Each is, we believe, a significant facet of school fight initiation and management. The first concerns the role of intruders or "unauthorized persons." The second focuses on the use of weapons, and the third concerns corporal punishment.

INTRUDERS

Intruders may be of several types: (a) persons who do not and never did attend the school, as in Incident 153; (b) persons who previously attended and who have either graduated, quit, or been suspended, as in Incident 154; or (c) persons who do attend school but are truant, internal dropouts (those who remain on school property but attend no classes), or roamers (those who show up for classes for which they are not registered), as in Incident 155. These persons are often youngsters with time on their hands and trouble in their hearts. They are often contributors to student-student fights and other forms of in-school and near-school aggression. School systems in the United States have begun employing a wide diversity of intruder management techniques to combat this problem, as listed in Table 3.

(153) At about 2:10 P.M., in front of the building, I noticed two students that didn't belong to the school. P. and T. started exchanging words with another student (H.) who goes to S. School. I told H. to go back inside the school, and I then closed the doors. I told P. and T. to leave. . . . I then watched them leave the property, headed towards the tennis court. The school officer then restated to them to keep going and to leave the property.

(154) At about 1:30 P.M. Tuesday, I was coming out of the office. I asked D. and a couple of students for a pass. She

TABLE 3

Management Techniques to Prevent School Intruders

1. Prepare and provide visitor regulation list.

2. Limit and monitor visitor entry and movement.

3. Employ student identification system.

4. Require visitor sign-in and badges.

5. Install alarms on infrequently used doors.

6. Register and sticker all staff and student cars.

7. Question and discourage loiterers.

said, "I don't have one—I am going to the counselor" and proceeded down the hall. I remembered then that she had been suspended. I went back into the office and asked if she was supposed to be here if she was suspended. They said she was not to be on the premises. I returned to the hall and asked her to come to the office. After a little yelling from her, she came down the hall and said, "What are they going to do, arrest me?" "Go get the cops," she said. I said, "Just go in the office like I asked," and she yelled out, "You can kiss my white ass" and went into the office.

(155) I was teaching a PE class seventh period when T. came into the class. I asked him to leave and told him I had a copy of his class schedule and that he was to go to his class listed on his schedule. T. refused, and I had to escort him out and lock the door behind him. Somehow he reentered, and I had to repeat the same process. I had also had the same problem second period with T. coming into the classroom. . . .

With about 2 minutes left in the period (seventh) I was supervising the class football game when I was blinded by some object. I went down on one knee and tried to regain my vision. When I was able to see again I asked the students what hit me, and they said some green ball. Several other students ran out of the class after the student who threw it . . . and caught him on the second floor. They brought him (T.) back downstairs, and Mr. K. and Mr. G. took him up to the office. I told them I would call the office in reference to the assault.

WEAPONS

Included in our pool of incidents were a substantial number of weapons reports. These weapons included guns of various types, knives, a screwdriver, a baseball bat, scissors, a large safety pin, and various other pointed objects. The two incidents we have selected both involve guns, one a shotgun brought in to "settle a score" with another student (Incident 156) and the other a pistol loaded with hollow-point bullets brought to school to "show off" (Incident 157).

(156) I was coming from lunch to go back to my room, and I had to pass by the front doors of the school, and I looked out and here was a student that I recognized. And he was walking up towards the front door, and he had a shotgun in his hand. And about that time the assistant principal passed me, and I said . . . there is so-and-so, and he has a shotgun. The assistant principal and I stood there at the door until this boy walked in, and he had this gun loaded, and he had it cocked, and he had his finger on the trigger, and he said, "I am going to kill somebody," and he started up the steps. And I can remember the assistant principal was on one side of this boy and I was on the other side, and we walked with him through one whole wing of the building. And it was like we were both just talking as fast as we could talk to this kid, having no idea of what we would do if he found who he was looking for. He went up to the fourth floor and walked all the way through that wing, and back down to the third floor, and back down to the first floor, and we walked with him the whole way. And he walked out of the building still with his

shotgun. The police had been called. They didn't get there until after he left, but he did leave with the shotgun. And the police went to his home. . . . I was young in teaching then and it was . . . really a scary kind of thing. And you wonder later, Well, why did we do that? Why did we walk with this kid? But I guess it's because there wasn't anything else to do. You couldn't just let him walk in with a shotgun. You didn't know what to do. You just go with him.

(157) On Friday, April 4, three students were arrested for possession of a deadly weapon on school grounds. Student 1 is a 13-year-old seventh grader who had never been in serious trouble. Student 2 is a 15-year-old learning disabled student who is in my self-contained classroom. . . . Student 3 is a 14-year-old emotionally disturbed student who is also in my self-contained program. . . .

Student 1 apparently stole a .22 caliber gun from his father. The gun was fully loaded with hollow-point bullets and did not have the safety on. Before the first class of the day, this gun was in the hands of all three students. The first student was showing off the gun to the second student. Student 2 said he was shocked that the other boy was showing the gun unconcealed. Student 2 removed his sweatshirt and wrapped the gun in it so other people would not catch a glimpse of the weapon. He then went to his hallway locker at 7:50 A.M. along with the rest of the school population. Student 3's locker is next to Student 2's locker and [Student 3] was aware that Student 2 was hiding something. According to Student 2, Student 3 asked him if it was a gun, to which Student 2 replied yes. Student 3 then asked or told Student 2 to give it to him to keep in his locker, at which Student 2 did. All students then went to first-period class. . . .

Meanwhile, a student caught a glimpse of the gun and reported what she saw to the principal. After searching many lockers of people who may have been involved, the weapon was found in Student 3's locker. . . . The principal asked me what class Student 3 was attending. I responded, "Gym class," at which he sent a hall monitor and myself to locate him and escort him to the office. . . .

By this time, the principal had found the other students involved and met with each student. . . . All three students were arrested by the . . . police and brought to the public safety building for possession of a deadly weapon. . . . I was also told that these teens would not be allowed back to . . . school ever [or] to the . . . school district until [the following year]. . . .

The police report later stated [Student 1] brought the weapon because boys were picking on him. . . .

Student 1's father was surprised that his son had his gun. Student 2's mother was somewhat shocked but is no stranger to having her sons in trouble. Two are currently in jail— one for murder, the other for drugs. Student 3's brother answered the call and laughed at the news.

Although neither gun was fired in these particular instances, the general proliferation of guns and other weaponry in the United States has begun to make some schools resemble armed camps. Youths claim that they acquire and carry guns for protection, because their enemies have guns, to "get" someone, to impress people, or because their friends have one. Schools have responded in a wide variety of ways to this threat. According to the National School Safety Center, those bringing guns to school have been reprimanded (16 percent), suspended (65 percent), or expelled (19 percent).[6] Reflecting the common school tendency to seek technological solutions to human problems, several schools employ environmental interventions to reduce the chance a student will bring a gun to school. The most popular of these interventions are listed in Table 4.

CORPORAL PUNISHMENT

Corporal punishment is still permitted in schools in 23 of the United States. The number of states in which corporal punishment is allowed has been declining steadily in recent decades, but in the last few years the decline has ceased and three state legislatures are in fact considering its reintroduction. Incident 158 is one example of a number of incidents reported in our pool. Two children fight and are sent to the principal. He gives each one "three licks" and sends them back to class. In much the same manner, although sometimes much

---
TABLE 4

Environmental Interventions for Gun Prevention

1. Use metal detectors and wands.

2. Remove student lockers.

3. Conduct locker/car searches.

4. Institute locker sharing between students and faculty.

5. Locate lockers opposite school office.

6. Enforce use of clear or mesh bookbags.

7. Establish weapons hot line.

---

more viciously, corporal punishment is meted out 700,000 times per year in America's schools. Such consequences are not distributed evenly geographically across the country. Ten of the 23 states that permit corporal punishment lie in the Southeast. Approximately 30 percent of America's schoolchildren are minority youngsters; they receive 40 percent of the corporal punishment. Children labeled learning disabled or behavior disordered also receive corporal punishment in schools disproportionate to their numbers.[7]

We totally and unequivocally oppose corporal punishment. It is, in our view, unethical, ineffective, and inappropriate in a civilized society. Its use teaches students that "might makes right" and thus directly or subtly encourages violence. Abused persons tend to pass abuse on. The effectiveness of corporal punishment in diminishing transgressive behavior tends to be temporary, often lasting only as long as the punishing person is present. Further, corporal punishment fails to teach youngsters more positive means for dealing the next time with the type of situation in which they got into trouble. If, as in Incident 158, the "licks" are for punching another youth who has been insulting, corporal punishment does not teach how to respond to the next insult by walking away, ignoring, assertion, diversion, or any other nonviolent means. Quite the opposite, it is likely to *increase* the chance that the next insult will also result in punching.

> (158) Two girls in my class had been arguing about each other's families. I had not heard the statements that led up to the first punch, but [they] concerned the "dead folk" in one of the girl's family. One girl got up and walked by the other's desk, and that led to the opportunity for the first punch. I did not see who struck whom first, but they started at it. I got up and pushed the two apart and stood between the two. I put my hand on each girl's back and walked them to my doorway. I called on the intercom that there had been a fight and I was sending the disputants up to the principal. He interviewed the girls and then gave each three licks and sent them back to class.

NOTES

1. R. Van Houten and D. M. Doleys, "Are social reprimands effective?" in S. Axelrod and J. Apsche (Eds.), *The effects of punishment on human behavior* (New York: Academic, 1983).

2. A. P. Goldstein, B. Harootunian, and J. C. Conoley, *Student aggression: Prevention, management, and replacement training* (New York: Guilford, 1994).

3. Goldstein et al., 1994.

4. F. A. Ianni, "The social organization of the high school: School specific aspects of school crime" in E. Wenk and N. Harlow (Eds.), *School crime and disruption* (Davis, CA: Responsible Action, 1978).

5. I. A. Spergel and G. D. Curry, *Survey of youth gang problems and programs in 45 cities and 6 sites* (Washington, DC: Office of Juvenile Justice and Delinquency Prevention).

6. National School Safety Center, *Disarming our schools* (Miami: Author, 1993).

7. Goldstein et al., 1994.

Physical Intervention

This chapter provides concrete, usable information about how to physically intervene with aggressive students. To accomplish this end, we cover a variety of topics that will enable educators to deal effectively and safely with violent situations. Such situations can be dangerous for all involved: The potential for injury exists not only for the teachers who intervene, but also for the students who are fighting and watching. Skilled use of the approaches in this chapter will greatly reduce the risk involved for all parties.

DEVELOPING AN INTERVENTION PLAN

Developing an intervention plan is the first step in a school's preparation for the fights that inevitably will occur. How such a plan is developed can be critical to its acceptance and implementation. In particular, the planning process should include actively soliciting the involvement of a wide range of interested parties. Parents, for example, are well within their rights to question the use of force by any school personnel. Most parents would support the idea that fights need to be stopped by anyone who is capable and close by. But it is important that there be a full airing and exchange of views about all the issues involved. Other community members such as the police may be valuable contributors to the planning effort. In some school settings, students may also be included.

The planning committee discusses and establishes policy to answer the following types of questions: What are acceptable methods for stopping fights? What types of postfight disciplinary measures are preferred? Should parents or students be encouraged to litigate or mediate after fights? and When does the school prosecute? All these questions and more should be discussed in a collaborative way and consensus reached among interested parties.

When a school develops an intervention plan, four organizing principles come into play. These concern personal safety, fight scene management, a team approach, and training.

Personal Safety

An overriding feature of a good intervention plan is its concern for personal safety. Any time a teacher is involved in breaking up a fight, he or she is at risk of being injured. Such risks are even greater if the teacher intervenes alone. As many of the incidents in chapter 2 illustrate, unilateral intervention efforts often fail, and the teacher ends up being hit or injured. So why do some teachers act alone in these high-risk situations? It is because teachers quite typically are caring people who feel responsible for their students and wish to prevent them from becoming injured.

This kind of concern for students is essential in teaching. However, teachers are well advised to adopt a team strategy before intervening in a potentially dangerous situation. Police officers call for backup, and no one thinks any less of them. Police officers work as a team, and that team approach is what reduces the potential for injury. Some situations you can handle yourself, especially at the elementary level. But if you have any doubts about your safety or ability, these doubts are probably your instinct for self-preservation telling you that you need help. Often you may have to stand back while one person is hurting another. But remember, you are not just standing there— you are waiting for assistance so you can be most effective.

Fight Scene Management

Once you have called for assistance and tried to defuse the fight scene, as described in chapter 2 (see Table 2), your first job is to *separate* the disputants. Specific methods for accomplishing this crucial initial step are described and illustrated in detail later in this chapter.

Sometimes well-intentioned teachers or other school personnel separate students only to have them start fighting again as they are sitting in the same room waiting for the principal or being walked down the same hall to the office of the school nurse or counselor. It is therefore important to *isolate* the participants from each other and any audience of their peers that could become a catalyst for more fighting. This goal is accomplished by escorting the participants separately to a place where they can be effectively isolated from each other. Often this is an administrator's office.

The person or persons who bring a student to the isolation area should use strategies and tactics to continue to *calm* the student. This does not mean that one person must follow through with the entire process. Often students are angry at the person who broke up the fight. A different person can intervene successfully at this point to conduct the interview to determine what factors led up to the fight. This could be the principal, assistant principal, counselor, another teacher, or another member of the school staff.

It is important to *supervise* the student throughout the entire process. At no time during the process should the student be left unattended. If unsupervised, the student may leave the area to seek out an adversary. You can supervise a student by waiting in the same room as the student or by waiting outside the room. Sometimes it helps to give a student some privacy when he or she is trying to calm down; however, it is important to keep the student in view.

After the immediate situation has cooled and the facts have been obtained through the interview process, mediation, counseling, and so forth can commence to *solve* the underlying problems.

A Team Approach

Throughout this book we have stressed that there is safety in numbers. But to implement a team approach effectively, you will require the cooperation of the persons with whom you work.

Imagine a group of teachers who wish to develop a general intervention plan for the eighth-grade wing they occupy. We will assume that they have already agreed, as a school, that student aggression needs to be addressed and that the parents and administrators trust the teachers to perform such a task. We will also assume that the school has no existing plan or security force in place. In this wing of the building there are seven classrooms. This means that at least seven teachers will be available for most of the day. During lunch periods there will be only four teachers and one hall monitor, who is available for an hour and a half.

The first thing the team needs to do is to examine its strengths and weaknesses. They have three male teachers and one female teacher who feel comfortable getting physically involved, two older female teachers who feel they could not or would not be willing to get physically involved, and one older male teacher who feels his role is academics only. The hall monitor will agree to help on a limited basis if the teachers ask.

Now the team knows who is capable of "hands on" duties and who is not. This helps a great deal because the team members can now assume clearly defined roles. The four staff members who are willing to intervene physically will take on as their primary function the fight scene management role. When an altercation occurs, they will provide the muscle to break up the fight and restrain the participants if necessary. The two older female teachers, along with the hall monitor, will serve as crowd control. Their primary role will be preventing an audience from developing. This function is often crucial in preventing a minor disturbance from escalating into a major problem.

The older male teacher, who is reluctant to help out by intervening physically, may be useful for special tasks, such as notifying the administration or calling for further help. Alternatively, he may simply have to be excluded altogether. Not everyone is comfortable dealing with violent situations. If this is the case, the person should not be alienated because of these preferences; instead, he or she should be encouraged to attend meetings and training sessions to stay informed about the plans you are making.

You should also designate one person as team leader. The leader should be willing to intervene physically in the fight. This person's responsibility is to direct the separation and restraint of the fighting students.

Training

Ongoing training is central to the success of any intervention plan. Mastery of the specific intervention and personal safety techniques presented in the following pages is one goal of training. But before you apply a single technique, it is important first to have a good grasp of how to evaluate the fight scene and how to use assertive verbal commands to avoid the need for physical intervention. However, because some conflicts will become violent, it is also important that training prepare you to think like a fighter and to determine which student to restrain in a fight situation.

Before discussing these aspects of training, we want to stress that, although fight situations have similarities, every fight is inherently different. Some fights are extremely easy to break up, even laughable. Others—for example, gang-related multiple fight scenarios—are so violent that breaking them up is a major task. Keep in mind, then, that absolutes are not applicable and that the techniques examined in this chapter must always be adapted to suit your own needs and circumstances.

Assessing the fight scene

When you first approach students who are fighting, do not act impulsively. Acting on impulse will only get you in trouble. Take the time to assess the situation quickly by taking the following steps.

Scanning for weapons. Determine whether the fighters have any kind of weapons. Depending upon your school environment, you should also scan for weapons in the possession of onlookers. If weapons are present, you will need to make a decision: Do you and your team back off and call the police, or do you intervene? This is a difficult question that can be answered only in the context of specific circumstances and your school's policy. If the weapons are not drawn and your team has sufficient force, perhaps you can intervene successfully. But if you are at all unsure of yourself, you should back off and call for the police. (We address the issue of weapons more fully later on in the chapter.)

Scanning onlookers for potential problems. Look for others who may jump in or start other fights. Doing so can allow you to direct teachers to those areas and quell any potential additional disturbances.

Scanning the physical surroundings. Look for furniture or any other obstructions that would prevent you from separating and restraining the fighters. Only by knowing where obstructions are can you work around them. Also look for any items in the area that students might pick up, throw, or otherwise employ as weapons. Knowing where these items are can prevent unnecessary injury and damage.

Scanning for blood. As a group, teenagers are increasingly being infected with HIV, the virus that causes AIDS, and other blood-borne diseases. If bleeding is occurring, back off and get your fight

147

kit. (We will describe the purpose and contents of the fight kit later in this chapter.)

Using assertive verbal commands

As a classroom teacher you have to be assertive in order to teach your class effectively, and successful teachers are typically assertive people. Assertive verbal commands are your first means of intervention. Try to get the parties to stop fighting through verbal commands before you intervene physically.

Your assertive commands will need to be stated clearly and specifically. Unfortunately, teachers often try to problem solve, discuss, or reason with combatants while they are fighting or are in the process of being separated. This rarely works. You cannot command students to stop fighting and discuss the problem at the same time. When students are enraged, they are unable to listen to anything but short phrases—and even hearing those is going to be difficult. Use their names, tell them what you want them to do, and tell them to do it *now*. Simple statements like "Stop," "Stop now," "Stop hitting," and "Stop fighting" are best.

Too often people assume that being assertive means being confrontational or raising your voice. On the contrary, being assertive is simply being direct and clear about what you want. However, you cannot be direct unless people can hear you. Sometimes in order to get students' attention, you must be emphatic. If a fight breaks out and the participants are having trouble hearing you, you will have to raise your voice accordingly.

The tone of voice you use when issuing commands should be neutral. If you sound angry, your angry tone may inflame the fight—at a minimum, it will slow the process of calming the disputants. By issuing directions in a neutral tone you won't be adding to the already aggressive atmosphere. Speaking in a calm voice can also lessen the chance that you will become a target for aggression.

Many students come from backgrounds in which a calm, rational approach is looked upon as weakness. To these students, people who are weak are "punks" who do not deserve respect. Punks cannot back up what they say, are poor fighters, and are not very tough. With students who hold these beliefs, we urge that you make your directives firm as well as calm. In short, your verbal strategies should reflect what is likely to get the desired response from the particular students involved.

Even if your verbal attempt to break up the fight fails, you still have the opportunity to be verbally assertive. If after separating fighting students you sense that the one you have separated is going to try to continue to fight, you can use statements like the following: "Hey, you won the fight. She's not going to want any more of you" or "Hey, you got the best of him. Now let the principal suspend him for what he did." These types of statements may help reduce the student's incentive to continue fighting. This incentive often consists of the sense that the one student did not get a chance to hit the other enough and peers will think he or she lost. Making the student feel that he or she won reduces the level of anger. Most of the time these assertions are exaggerations. But if they convince the participant that there is no more need to fight, who cares? Your goal is to end the fight.

Thinking like a fighter

If your verbal commands fail to stop the fight and you have decided to intervene physically, you will need to be sure that you have sufficient assistance (e.g., that you are making use of a team approach), that you are not acting on impulse, and that you have evaluated the situation for weapons, obstructions, onlookers, and so forth, as suggested earlier.

You will also need to realize that once you initiate your procedure for physically breaking up a fight, you become an active participant in that fight. Because you are a participant, you will need to think like a fighter. You will need to understand and use the basic principles fighters use to protect themselves:

- Keep your hands up.
- Stay light on your feet.
- Maintain a proper stance.
- Keep your eyes open.
- Block the left and be ready for the right.
- Be aware of striking distance.

Following these suggestions can greatly reduce your risk of injury while at the same time increasing your chances of successfully breaking up the fight.

Once you have decided to intervene physically, you should approach the fighters with a full commitment to breaking up the fight. If you operate at half speed, you will not be able to stop the fight and may get hurt. If you attempt to restrain a student with a poor grip because you are uncertain, he or she may be able to get away and fight again. You will then have to break the fight up a second time and risk injury twice.

Determining which combatant to approach

If you do decide physical intervention is necessary, before you apply any specific technique, you will need to decide which fighter to approach. This will depend in part on your own and your team's abilities. If you are a lightly built 120 pounds, you probably do not want to choose an out-of-control 180-pound athlete. Some of you may have had success restraining students larger than yourself, but chances are special circumstances permitted you to do so. Generally, then, your size and skill will determine which student to approach. Also relevant are whether or not you and the student know each other and, if you do, the quality of that relationship.

A common debate concerns whether or not to approach the apparent loser or the apparent winner when you are in a situation in which you must intervene alone. Some feel that you should attempt to restrain the person who appears to be losing. Their view is that if you restrain the person who is winning, the person who is losing may take advantage of the situation to go back after the winner. If, on the other hand, you restrain the person who is losing, the person who is winning will presumably be less likely to use that opportunity to sneak in a few more shots. The assumption is that because that person was winning, he or she will be easier to calm down.

Proponents of the opposing view suggest that attempting to restrain the winner is actually the safer option. Persons with this view believe that by restraining the winner you can effectively stop the fight entirely. Obviously, if you grab the student who is throwing the punches, the fight ends. If the losing student then attempts to come after the winning student, you can threaten to turn the winner loose on the loser. It is presumed that this threat will limit the loser's desire to continue fighting.

The problem with both of these schools of thought is that an enraged student's responses are extremely unpredictable. We can guess and we can assume, but we can't guarantee behavior during these situations. How can you predict that if you restrain the loser the winner won't want to continue hitting the loser even more? By restraining the loser, you may be setting him or her up for more injury. What if you restrain the winner and your threats about releasing him or her fail to impress the loser? If you are forced to release the winner in his or her own self-defense, you will have to break up the fight a second time. You must also consider whether or not a strategy that relies on intimidation and the muscle of the winner is justifiable.

Many times, teachers choose to separate fighting students by restraining the one they know best and who will therefore presumably listen. It makes sense to try to deal with a student with whom you are familiar, especially if you have to calm the student down during isolation or after. This is obviously a better choice than trying to deal with an enraged student whom you do not know. Trust and rapport may be the crucial factor in ending the situation.

The strategy of restraining the student who is the most aggressive and cannot stop fighting is also commonly adopted. The most aggressive student is not necessarily the one who is winning. Rather, it is the student who is so enraged that he or she is determined to keep fighting the opponent or anyone else who gets in the way. The rationale for this choice is that the most aggressive fighter is creating a very volatile atmosphere that may result in serious injury—and subduing him or her will result in the greatest gain. Unfortunately, unless there is sufficient help, restraining a student this angry and aggressive is dangerous to both student and teacher. Students that become this enraged often end up in a restraint situation that requires the help of other staff.

Yet another answer to the question of who should be restrained is no one! Some teachers and administrators believe that unless a student is an unwilling participant, a fight should not be stopped. Proponents of this view argue that interfering with a fight only prevents a natural pecking order from developing. They also suggest that this natural pecking order actually prevents fights because students "know their place." The students know whom they can and cannot start trouble with. The problem with this approach is obvious: Pecking orders are self-serving, and if the strong feel like picking on the weak, nothing prevents them from doing so. Bullying is frequent enough without receiving official sanction from school personnel.

A final consideration in determining which student to restrain concerns the student's sex: There are those who say, "You can't put your hands on a female student, no matter what." Realistically, the charge of inappropriate touching or sexual abuse does not apply when you are breaking up a bloody battle between girls or between girls and boys. Although extreme actions have been threatened, we have yet to read or hear about any male teacher's being fired or sued after breaking up a fight by physically restraining a female student. Whether they are male or female, when students are fighting, they are fighting. Your objective is to break up that fight.

PHYSICAL INTERVENTION TECHNIQUES

Restraint of students, defined broadly as any form of physical intervention in a fight situation, is controversial in some school districts. Our view is that the regulations governing such behavior by school personnel in New York State (where we all teach) are correct and to be generally recommended. In New York, one can restrain a student if the student is, at the time, a danger to self, others, or property. These regulations provide a standard for when restraint is legally permissible; they do not mean that one must restrain a student under such circumstances. We believe that restraint within these parameters is reasonable when done properly.

When no other means are effective, restraint is a means to safely control dangerous, aggressive behavior before someone gets hurt— nothing more, nothing less. It is not a means of instruction or an aspect of a school's curriculum or discipline code. We do not condone the use of restraint as a means of discipline or as a consequence for inappropriate behavior.

Proper technique is the key. People who view physical intervention as undesirable probably have witnessed improper use of restraint or situations where students have been injured through poor technique. If they have, then their feelings are understandable. Although such interventions can appear harmful, when proper technique is used, the risk of injury is minimal.

As with many new skills, the techniques described and illustrated on the following pages may seem a little awkward at first. Take the time to learn the techniques as they are presented until you feel comfortable with their use. When you practice with your team, keep in mind that you want to help one another learn the techniques. Give very little resistance at first; make each other look good when practicing and go with the flow until you are comfort-able with the movements. Then gradually add resistance to make the situation more realistic. Depending on your group's composi-tion and level of comfort with the skills, you may want to enlist the help of a professional familiar with carrying out safe restraints.

Angle of Approach

You should always move toward the combatants with what fighters refer to as a proper *angle of approach*. This allows you to approach with some degree of safety. Determine the angle of approach by taking into account (a) the current position of the students, (b) the striking distance, and (c) the physical surroundings.

Whether the students are locked up on the ground, standing up in a bear hug, or trading blows as though in a boxing ring, one angle of approach usually works well—a 45-degree angle from the left or right of the fighter's center, approaching from behind (Figure 1).

Figure 1

You might be tempted to assume that if you approach the fighter directly from behind you will be able to use that person as a shield. But what if the fighter moves to duck a punch before you can restrain him or her? Then you take the blow. When you are directly behind the person, you are right in the line of fire. But if you approach from behind at the 45-degree angle, you are to the side of the opponent's punches and can more easily move out of the way if you have to. You can protect yourself and still initiate a restraint technique from behind, where you

Figure 2

have more control. It is also less likely that the fighter you are approaching will land on you if he or she falls backward before you get control of the situation.

While you are approaching from the 45-degree angle, you will need to be aware of the position of your hands and feet. Your hands should be held high at about shoulder level (Figure 2). Keeping your hands up allows you to keep your head covered and block any blows that might come your way. This is the best position when students are trading blows in any position. If they are locked up on the ground, you should still approach from a 45-degree angle. In this case, however, the danger is that you will be hit in the groin or knee by a struggling student's feet or elbows. This generally happens when one student is trying to kick the other and misses or when one student rolls the other over and legs fly in the air. So instead of keeping your hands up, keep them down in front of the groin area, using a closed-fist position (Figure 3).

Figure 3

Besides maintaining proper hand position, it is important to approach the fight with your weak leg forward and strong leg back, in what is called a *toe-heel position* (Figures 2 and 3). Your shoulders and hips should be angled slightly sideways and your knees slightly bent. This position allows you to move quickly and with solid balance. Keeping your balance can help you avoid being knocked down and evade any blows.

Figure 4

As you approach the fighters, keep in mind the *striking distance* (Figure 4). This is the distance required for one person to hit another. If you enter that range unprepared, you are inviting injury. It is important to make sure that you get your hands up (or down, if students are locked up on the ground) and maintain a proper stance before entering the striking distance.

The last consideration in determining the angle of approach involves the *physical surroundings*. You do not want to trip over something and get hurt before you even begin to intervene in the fight. You also want to keep the environment in mind because when you do get the disputants separated, you will want to have a clear path to escort them away from the scene.

Separation Techniques

Many fights involve a situation where two students are locked up in a bear hug, standing position or in a headlock position on the floor. The task here is to get the students to release their grip so you can pull them apart.

155

Finger Release

This procedure requires some practice but is easy to learn and implement and is generally safe for you and the students involved.

1. With your weaker hand, grab the student's forearm as best you can (Figure 5).

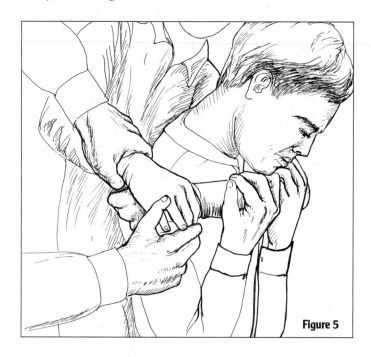

Figure 5

2. Using your stronger hand, grab the student's small finger and ring finger and bend them back toward the back of the hand. Very little force is needed, so don't be overzealous and injure the student's fingers.

3. Once the student's hold is broken, release the fingers and transfer your grip to the student's arm.

4. Pull the student away and institute an appropriate restraint maneuver.

Grab, Smother, and Lift

This technique is useful in a situation where you are able to handle one opponent while your partner handles the other. It works best when the student's arms are positioned so that you can pin them against his or her sides in one motion.

1. Use the standard 45-degree approach.

2. At the last moment, slide behind your target and move both of your arms downward to "smother" the student's arms against his or her sides (Figure 6.1).

Figure 6.1

3. Make sure your head is to the side of the student's to prevent being head-butted (Figure 6.2).

4. Begin to move the student backward and away from the scene, using a good, balanced stance. If the student is much smaller than you are, you can lift him or her off of the ground as you move backward. This can prevent you from falling but is only effective if you are bigger than the student.

Figure 6.2

157

Two-Person Arm Grab

This technique is used by two team members on one combatant. The technique is very effective on larger students but can be used on smaller youngsters as well. The technique also allows you to initiate the Two-Person Backward Walk, a type of a controlled escort, immediately after the separation. (This and other specific escort techniques are discussed later in the chapter.)

1. Use the standard 45-degree angle approach from behind. (The following instructions assume you are approaching from the student's right.)

2. Approach the student with your right leg forward, which also means your right hand is forward (Figure 7.1). (Your partner approaches from the left side and performs the following steps simultaneously.)

3. With your forward hand, try to grab or hook the student's forearm, using a downward motion.

4. Now grab the student's lower forearm with your other hand and slide your forward arm underneath the student's upper arm (Figure 7.2). The student's upper arm should now rest in the crook between your biceps and your forearm. You should not be chest to chest.

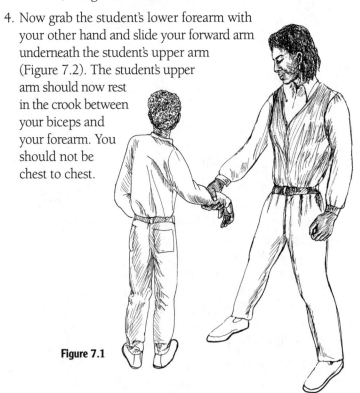

Figure 7.1

Figure 7.2

5. Push the student's wrist and forearm into your chest area (Figure 7.3). Simultaneously and with equal pressure, pull back with your bent arm. This safely locks the student's arm and limits any type of hitting.

6. At this point you and your partner can initiate the Two-Person Backward Walk, if necessary.

Figure 7.3

Crossed-Arm Pin

This is a good technique to use when a physical intervention requires only two persons (plus crowd control).

1. Use the standard 45-degree angle approach. Move behind the student as in the Grab, Smother, and Lift maneuver.

2. As you reach around the student from behind, grab the student's left lower forearm with your right hand and right lower forearm with your left (Figure 8.1).

3. Pull the student's arms (which are now crossed) tightly against his or her body. Slide forward into the student's body with your strong side forward. Your forward shoulder should be right next to the student's back (Figure 8.2).

4. Keep your head to one side of the student's head or low in the student's shoulder area to keep from being head-butted.

Figure 8.1

Figure 8.2

5. To keep control of the student, lean into the student and simultaneously pull back on his or her arms. Do not stand flat-footed; maintain your mobility by staying up on the balls of your feet. Adjust your foot position as the student tries to move.

Four-Person Pull Apart

This technique is used to pull apart two combatants in a locked-up position. We will discuss two variations of the technique, one for when the opponents are on the ground and one for when they are standing up.

VARIATION A: COMBATANTS ON THE GROUND

For purposes of illustration, the figures for Variation A show two team members executing the maneuver on one combatant. Two additional team members simultaneously perform the same operation on the other combatant.

1. Use the standard 45-degree angle of approach. Because the students are on the ground, you will need to hold your arms low to cover your groin area (Figure 9.1).

Figure 9.1

Close your fists to prevent having your fingers jammed by a kick. You can also turn your leg inward and expose your hip to cover the groin area.

2. If necessary, break the students' grips, using the procedure already described for breaking strong grips (Figure 9.2).

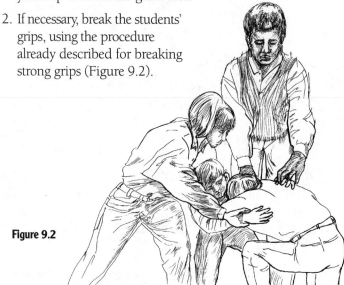

Figure 9.2

3. Once grips are sufficiently broken, get control of the opponents' arms (Figure 9.3). You can do this in one of two ways:

   ▪ Grip the upper arm and lower forearm. This two-position grab counteracts any excess movement that can stress joints. If you have hold of just the lower forearm, the student can easily bend at the elbow joint and perhaps twist free or dislocate the arm. The two-position grip is much safer.

   ▪ Use the Two-Person Arm Grab.

4. Once you have control of both combatants' arms, pull the combatants apart simultaneously.

VARIATION B: COMBATANTS STANDING UP

1. Approach the students, using the standard 45-degree angle.

2. Break students' grips as needed.

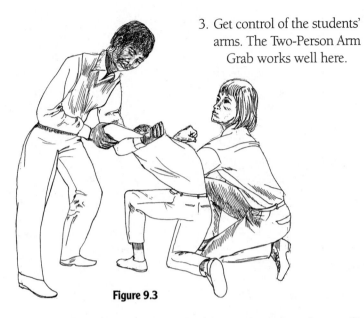

3. Get control of the students'
   arms. The Two-Person Arm
   Grab works well here.

Figure 9.3

4. Communicate to the team that everyone is ready to pull
   apart and do so when ready (Figure 10).

When you have four team members working to separate two
persons, you have a total of six participants in a fight situation that

Figure 10

is probably characterized by a good deal of aggression. With this number of people involved, the potential exists for things to go wrong. You may not be able to undo the fighters' grips, or in the confusion you may mistakenly grab your teammate's arm instead of the student's. The most frequent problem concerns miscommunication about when it is time to pull apart: Two team members pull one student before the other two team members are ready, and you all fall together in a big heap. If this happens, it is best for team members to move away from the fighters, regroup, and start again.

Better team communication through a team leader is essential in situations like these. The team leader initiates the different steps in the break-up to synchronize everyone's timing and ensure that the team works together. Practice is necessary to maintain an adequate level of skill in complex fight situations. Role-playing such scenarios will make it easier to contend with real events.

Torso Shoulder Lock

Sometimes fighters are so tightly interwoven that you cannot get hold of their arms. This technique allows you to get a better hold when you are having difficulty pulling one person away from the other. In it, one team member immobilizes the fighter's body and one of his or her arms; a second team member controls the student's free arm. If four team members are available, the other pair might apply this same technique to the second combatant.

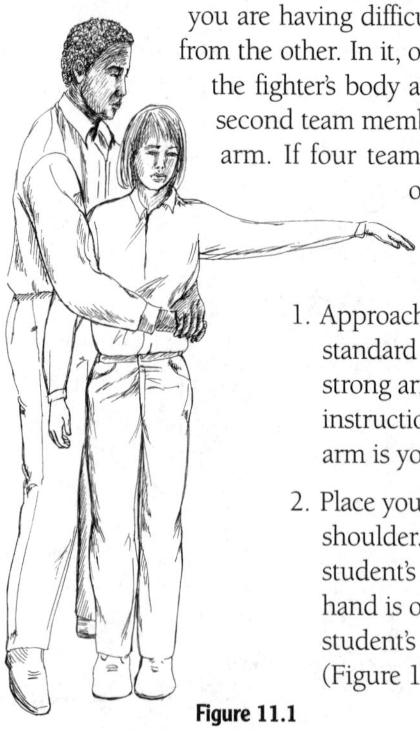

1. Approach the situation, using the standard 45-degree angle. Keep your strong arm forward. (The following instructions assume that your strong arm is your right.)

2. Place your right arm over the student's shoulder. Continue down across the student's chest so that your right hand is on the upper left side of the student's rib cage, by the left armpit (Figure 11.1).

Figure 11.1

164

3. Come underneath with your left hand from behind and grab your own right wrist (Figure 11.2).

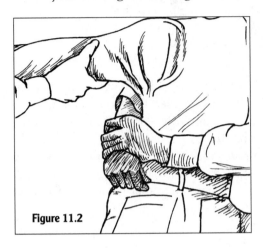

Figure 11.2

4. Position the front of your right shoulder against the student's right shoulder and pull tightly, keeping a wide stance for balance. Stay on the original 45-degree angle to keep your head away from the student's.

5. Have your partner control the left arm using a two-point hold (Figure 11.3). Alternatively, your partner could use the method illustrated for the Two-Person Arm Grab.

Figure 11.3

Make certain when doing this procedure that you place your arms underneath the student's armpit and not around the neck. Otherwise, the hold turns into a headlock, which is very dangerous and can result in choking.

Wall Pin

The Wall Pin is useful when two students are fighting and one of them is against the wall or in a corner. In this situation the wall prevents you from restraining both fighters. When you pull the fighter on the outside away, the one against the wall is free to take advantage of the situation to attack again. This technique helps you prevent this from happening by using the wall to your advantage. The following instructions assume that other team members have restrained the fighter on the outside.

VARIATION A: ONE TEAM MEMBER

1. Work with your weak side forward and strong side back. (The following instructions assume that this is left forward, right back.) This allows your strong leg to support you against the student.

2. Keep your left hip into the student as you place your arms around his or her arms and body (Figure 12).

3. Pull in tightly, using your legs and shoulder to pin the student to the wall. The student can be held in this position until you can escort.

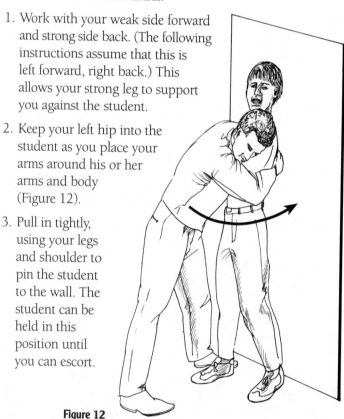

Figure 12

Figure 13.1

VARIATION B: TWO TEAM MEMBERS

1. Two team members quickly move in on the target student. The team member on the left grabs the student's right arm, and the team member on the right grabs the student's left arm (Figure 13.1).

2. If you are on the student's left, place your left shoulder into the student's shoulder and chest area as you start your grab. (If you are on the right, reverse these instructions.)

3. Your grab consists of an arm restraint like the one employed in the Two-Person Arm Grab. If you are on the student's left, place your left arm underneath the student's triceps area, hooking it between your biceps and forearm. Then grab the student's lower forearm with your right hand. (If you are on the right, reverse these instructions.)

4. Hold the student's arm firmly in place as you push slightly forward with your body. This will effectively trap the arm. When done in conjunction with your partner, the student can be pinned into the wall and safely held (Figure 13.2).

Figure 13.2

Restraint Techniques

In its narrower sense, *restraint* refers to that specific set of techniques used to control students after they have been separated in a fight situation. Safety—both yours and the student's—is a primary concern when using the restraint techniques described in the following pages.

You should first be sure that the student is capable of breathing freely. You will need to monitor carefully the amount of weight being exerted upon the student, particularly around the chest area. We would like to suggest that you avoid putting any weight at all on the chest area, but in some circumstances you cannot avoid putting some weight on the upper torso. Especially with smaller children, you will need to be aware of the amount of pressure you are putting on the chest. You should never cover the student's face for any reason, even if the person is spitting or biting. Simply keeping the student face down is an effective way to prevent these behaviors. Another thing you should avoid is restraining a person on soft furniture or cushions. Even if using a soft area will prevent bruises and scrapes, the risk of suffocation is too great. Cushions conform to a person's body; they can also conform to the face and block the nose and mouth, preventing the person from breathing. It is much safer to restrain a person on a hard or firm surface.

Next, you will need to be aware of pain. This does not refer to the pain you may experience from banging your knee or elbow on the floor, but rather to pain as a means of physically controlling someone. The Finger Release technique for dealing with strong grips does involve some discomfort, but if cautiously used the technique is justifiable. Otherwise, you simply cannot inflict pain as a means to control a student. We have seen teachers twist arms; bend wrists; bend arms behind students' backs; and hit, squeeze, and pinch students as a means of control. These are not appropriate teacher behaviors for restraint or any other purpose. Restraint is a means to contain aggressive behavior safely, *without* causing pain or injury.

In addition to ensuring that the person can breathe and that you are not using pain as a means of control, several other concerns are relevant to the effective use of restraint:

- Be careful not to twist elbows, wrists, or knees. Avoid excessive pressure that could cause dislocation of joint areas. Always try to keep a firm grip on two points of a limb or in the center of a limb.

- Be aware of rug and floor burn. The more a person can move around on the floor, the more easily these injuries can occur.

- Respect the person being restrained. Always consider how that person is feeling (often embarrassed). Never belittle or make sarcastic comments. This will only enrage the person further and make the restraint much more difficult.

- Keeping the person face down always works better. You can keep a person more stable in this position and prevent him or her from spitting or biting. The face-down position also prevents excess mucus and saliva (often present when a student is enraged) from interfering with breathing.

Levels of aggression

Depending on the severity of the aggression, different restraint techniques will be necessary.

Level 1: Low-level aggression

It is necessary to place your hands on the student to prevent the student from moving. You are blocking a person's path who is not really resisting you; at the same time, you are perhaps placing a hand or hands on the person's shoulders or arms (Figure 14).

Figure 14

Level 2: Midlevel aggression

One person remains standing and restrains the student. The situation requires that you actively hold the student with a single-person restraint technique (Figure 15).

Figure 15

170

Level 3: High-level aggression

In cases in which a student will not calm down quickly, multiple restrainers hold the student upright or prone. A peer audience may be present but is easily controlled (Figure 16).

Figure 16

Level 4: Extreme aggression

At this level, the situation is accompanied by the threat of other students fighting or getting involved in the restraint in a negative way. Multiple restrainers are involved, and active crowd control/security is needed (Figure 17).

Figure 17

171

Standing arm locks

These first two restraint techniques are useful when a single person must control one combatant who is exhibiting Level 2 aggression. Very effective if put into effect immediately after you have separated two fighters, these techniques can be used on just about anyone as long as you are physically capable of applying them. This does not mean that you have to be exceptionally strong, but, as with all of the techniques described, you will need to practice to become proficient in their application.

Triceps Lock

1. Approach from behind at the standard 45-degree angle.

2. Hook your left arm underneath the student's left arm with your palm facing the student's back (Figure 18.1). Simultaneously hook your right arm underneath the student's right arm with your palm facing the student's back.

3. Continue sliding your hands across the student's back, placing your palms down over the student's triceps (Figure 18.2).

Figure 18.1

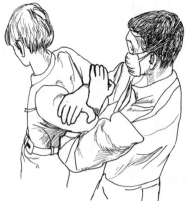

4. Keep one leg forward and one leg back for balance. Lean slightly into the student. Keep your head to one side to avoid being head-butted.

Figure 18.2

Double Arm Lock

1. Approach at the standard 45-degree angle from behind.

2. Place your left arm underneath the student's left arm, palm out, then reach over to grab the student's right biceps area (Figure 19.1).

Figure 19.1

Figure 19.2

3. Simultaneously reach your right arm around the student's chest and pull in (Figure 19.2).

4. Keep one foot forward and one back for balance. Keep your head to one side to keep yourself from being head-butted.

In both of these one-on-one restraint techniques, room for error exists. The more you practice these skills, the easier it will be to apply them. Even though you practice, you still might get your foot stepped on, be bitten or scratched, or even catch a head-butt. There is not much you can do to prevent students from attempting to counter your restraint: To deal with a student who can bend his or her wrist and scratch you, you could move your grip up a little farther on the arm. The higher grip will effectively keep your hand out of reach of the student's fingers. To help keep from getting your feet stepped on, keep moving them or be prepared to move them as needed. To avoid head-butts, keep your head to one side. To prevent biting, try to keep your arms and hands away from the combatant's mouth. The best thing is to be prepared for these behaviors so you can deal with them effectively if they occur.

Crossed-arm techniques

The following two techniques are useful in a one-on-one situation in which the combatant is exhibiting Level 3 aggression. The first, the sitting version, is best for elementary or younger middle school students. The second is more appropriate for older, larger students.

Sitting Crossed-Arm Restraint

1. Get behind the student as you would when doing the Crossed-Arm Pin.

2. Lean into the student for control and maneuver your back against a wall (Figure 20.1).

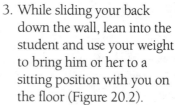

Figure 20.1

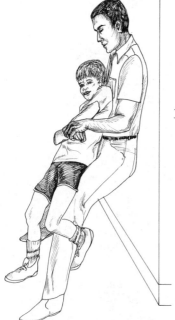

3. While sliding your back down the wall, lean into the student and use your weight to bring him or her to a sitting position with you on the floor (Figure 20.2).

Figure 20.2

4. Get control of the student's legs by wrapping your legs around the student's (Figure 20.3). You can either cross your ankles, place your feet firmly on the floor, or weave them around the student's ankles.

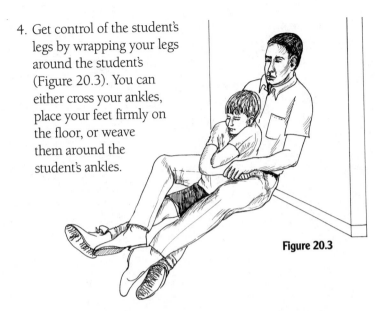

Figure 20.3

5. Keep your head to either the left or the right side of the student's to avoid being head-butted.

Standing Crossed-Arm Restraint

1. Grab the student's left lower forearm with your right hand (Figure 21.1).

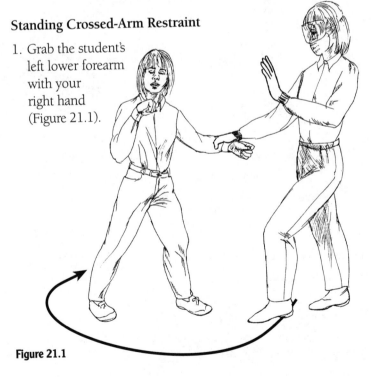

Figure 21.1

2. With your left foot first, step around the student's right side until you are behind the student (Figure 21.2).

3. Reach around the student's left side with your left hand to grab the student's right lower forearm (Figure 21.3).

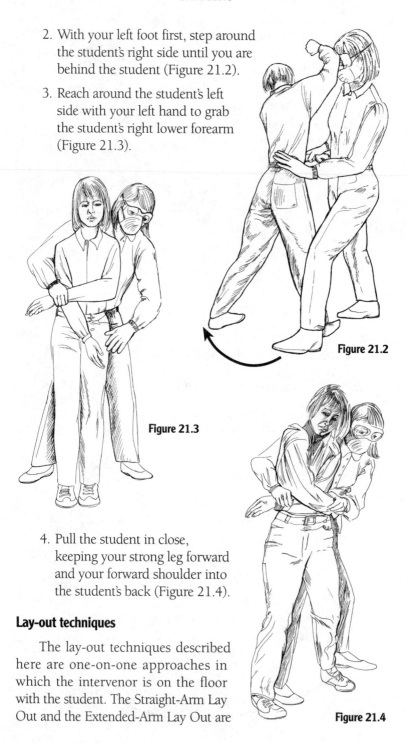

Figure 21.2

Figure 21.3

4. Pull the student in close, keeping your strong leg forward and your forward shoulder into the student's back (Figure 21.4).

Lay-out techniques

The lay-out techniques described here are one-on-one approaches in which the intervenor is on the floor with the student. The Straight-Arm Lay Out and the Extended-Arm Lay Out are

Figure 21.4

appropriate for use with a student who is exhibiting Level 3 aggression; the Scissors Lay Out can be used with a student who is less aggressive or who requires extended restraint.

Your first concern in using these techniques is getting the student to the floor safely. You want to avoid taking a student down on the floor face first. The student's face might hit the floor with his or her own body weight and yours following it. This could lead to rug or floor burns, as well as to more serious injury. If at all possible, you should take the student to the floor by first bringing him or her to a seated position, then initiating the lay out. One way to do this is by "smothering" the student's arms to his or her sides (as in the Grab, Smother, and Lift), then using your weight to bring the student to a seated position. The Crossed-Arm Pin is another effective approach to get to the floor position. These maneuvers work best with elementary or younger middle school students.

With larger students, you can use a form of take-down known as a Leg Block. This technique involves getting the student off balance by blocking the leg, pushing the upper body backward, then guiding the student to the floor by pulling up on the inside of the student's arm. If you have ever wondered how students of Judo weather so many falls during practice without injury, it is because they protect each other in this way. Instead of letting the opponent fall with full force to the floor, they control the impact by pulling up on the opponent's arm before the opponent hits the floor. The same principle applies in using the Leg Block: The more you pull up on the student before the student hits the ground, the less severe the impact.

Leg Block

1. Step forward with your right leg, placing your right leg behind the student's right leg. Keep your calf pressed tightly against the student's calf (Figure 22.1).

Figure 22.1

2. Hold the student's upper right arm in your left hand and place your right arm across the student's chest, with your right hand on the student's left shoulder area (Figure 22.2).

Figure 22.2

3. Pull the student's left arm toward you as you push the student's right shoulder away with your right hand (Figure 22.3). Simultaneously turn your hips to the left.

Figure 22.3

4. Pull up with your left hand as the student falls (Figure 22.4).

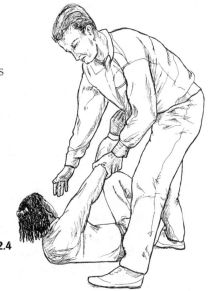

Figure 22.4

Straight-Arm Lay Out

1. To roll the student onto his or her stomach, orient your body perpendicular to the student's on the floor (Figure 23.1). (The following instructions assume that you are on the student's right.)

Figure 23.1

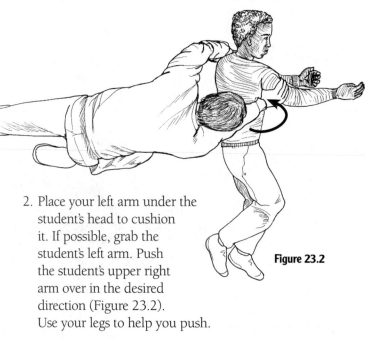

Figure 23.2

2. Place your left arm under the
   student's head to cushion
   it. If possible, grab the
   student's left arm. Push
   the student's upper right
   arm over in the desired
   direction (Figure 23.2).
   Use your legs to help you push.

3. Place the student's arms against his or her sides as you
   straddle the student's body with your knees. The student's arms will end up locked between your inner
   thighs and the student's own body (Figure 23.3).

4. Hook your feet inside the student's legs at about knee
   level to prevent the student from
   kicking you. If you cannot
   do this, place your
   hands behind your
   back to protect
   yourself from
   kicks.

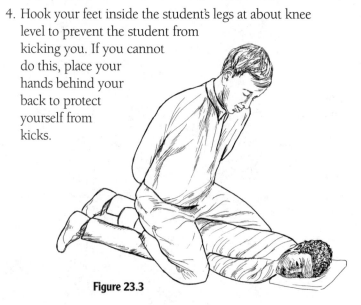

Figure 23.3

Sometimes enraged kids will try to bang their heads on the floor when in this position. If so, put one arm or hand underneath the student's forehead to cushion the blows. If this is too painful for you, you will need to use some sort of padding. A tightly rolled up shirt or a *head pad* is effective. About a foot square, a head pad is a rigid piece of closed-cell foam that can be placed underneath a student's head. This material is very dense and will not block breathing by conforming to a person's face. You can make your own head pad by purchasing and cutting up a camping mattress made from closed-cell foam. This material, used to make gardening mats, is also available at hardware stores. The head pad should be stored next to your fight kit (described later in this chapter).

Extended-Arm Lay Out

1. Complete Steps 1 and 2 as described for the Straight-Arm Lay Out.

2. Hold the student's mid- or lower forearms and extend each forearm outward at a 45-degree angle from the student's upper body. (Holding the mid- or lower forearm reduces the risk of injuring the elbow or shoulder area.)

3. Straddle the student's body with your knees, placing your shins over his or her legs (Figure 24).

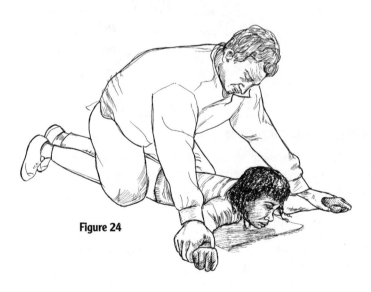

Figure 24

Scissors Lay Out

This technique can be used when a student is somewhat calm but requires extended restraint by one person. It works best for elementary or younger middle school students. You can also switch to this technique if you are fatigued from the other lay-out maneuvers.

1. Complete Steps 1 and 2 as described for the Straight-Arm Lay Out.

2. Place your weak leg underneath the student's hip area and your strong leg on top. (The following instructions assume that your strong leg is your right and that you are to the left of the student.)

3. Extend the student's left forearm out with your right arm, keeping the arm perpendicular to the student's body (Figure 25).

Figure 25

Multiple restraint techniques

Multiple restraint techniques involve two or more restrainers. These techniques are usually used for Level 3 and Level 4 situations, in which there is an intense display of aggression.

Two-Person Lay Out

This maneuver is a variation on the single-person lay-out techniques described earlier.

VARIATION A: STUDENT'S ARMS EXTENDED

1. Roll the student onto his or her stomach as directed in Steps 1 and 2 of the Straight-Arm Lay Out.

2. First team member: Straddle the student from a kneeling position at mid- to lower torso level (Figure 26).

Figure 26

3. First team member: Extend the student's arms forward at a 45-degree angle while gripping the student's mid- or lower forearm area.

4. Second team member: At the same time, lie across the backs of the student's legs.

VARIATION B: STUDENT'S ARMS PINNED

1. Roll the student onto his or her stomach as directed in Steps 1 and 2 of the Straight-Arm Lay Out.

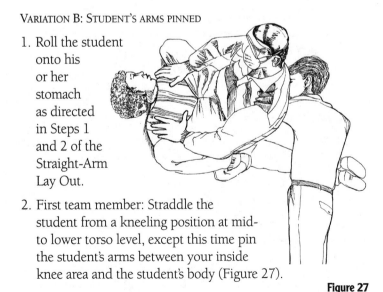

2. First team member: Straddle the student from a kneeling position at mid- to lower torso level, except this time pin the student's arms between your inside knee area and the student's body (Figure 27).

Figure 27

3. Second team member: At the same time, lie across the backs of the student's legs.

Three-Person Lay Out

1. Roll the student onto his or her stomach as directed in Steps 1 and 2 of the Straight-Arm Lay Out.

2. First team member (on the student's left): Extend the student's left arm. Rest the side of your body on the student's upper arm and control the mid- or lower forearm with your hands if needed (Figure 28).

Figure 28

3. Second team member (on the student's right): Repeat Step 2 on the student's right side.

4. Third team member: Lie across the lower back or upper leg area. Position yourself according to the student's size and level of aggressiveness: In general, positioning yourself too low on the legs will allow movement in the torso area, and the student may twist free or be more difficult to manage.

Four-Person Lay Out

1. Roll the student onto his or her stomach as directed in Steps 1 and 2 of the Straight-Arm Lay Out.

2. Two team members extend the student's arms, as in Steps 2 and 3 of the Three-Person Lay Out.

3. Third team member: Lie across the student's lower back or upper leg area (Figure 29).

4. Fourth team member: Lie across the student's lower leg area. Be sure to position your head in the direction opposite that assumed by the third team member.

Figure 29

Rollover

This maneuver allows four team members to bring a student to the floor, safely turn him or her over, and initiate the Four-Person Lay Out as a form of restraint.

1. Two team members approach the student from the sides, one on each side (Figure 30.1). Two others stay close by to assist.

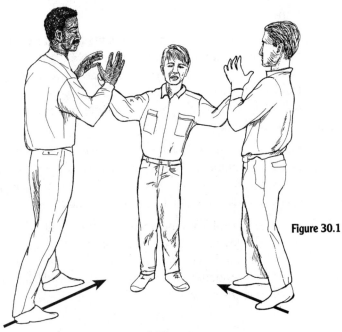

Figure 30.1

185

Figure 30.2

2. First team member (on the student's right): Using your outside hand, grab the student's upper arm area (Figure 30.2). Use your inside hand to grab the student's front shoulder area.

3. Second team member (on the student's left): At the same time, grab the student's lower arm with your outside hand and his or her front shoulder area with your inside hand. Grabbing the student's lower instead of upper arm will allow the first team member adequate room to apply the Leg Block.

4. First team member: Initiate the Leg Block, described earlier. Remember to keep your calf against the student's calf. (The second team member can do the same thing if needed. Most often, one Leg Block is sufficient.)

5. First and second team members: Together, push the student backward while pulling up on the student's arms to soften the fall. Your inside hand pushes on the front of the student's shoulder or chest as your hips and legs turn in the direction of the fall (Figure 30.3).

Figure 30.3

6. First and second team members: Lie across the student's arms (Figure 30.4).

7. Third team member: Lie across the student's upper leg area. Your head should be at the student's right side.

8. Fourth team member: Lie across the student's lower legs. Your head should be at the student's left side.

Figure 30.4

Figure 30.5

9. First team member: Place the student's right arm against his or her right side. Then move your body away, kneeling perpendicular to the student (Figure 30.5).

10. Second, third, and fourth team members: Assume a kneeling position perpendicular to the student, then roll the student over at the team leader's count of three (Figure 30.6).

   ▪ Second team member: Push the student's arm across his or her chest, simultaneously lifting and turning the student's shoulder in the direction of travel.

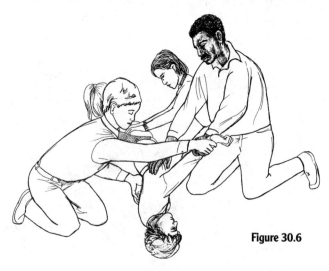

Figure 30.6

- Third team member (at upper leg area): Push the student's legs in the direction of travel.

- Fourth team member (at lower leg area): Pull the student toward you, in the direction of travel.

11. Initiate the Four-Person Lay Out (Figure 30.7).

Figure 30.7

Release Techniques

Sometimes releasing a student from restraint is as simple as letting the person up. However, a number of considerations are important in carrying out a safe and successful release.

Team communication

Designate one person to communicate with the student during any form of restraint. As already discussed, angry students are not going to process information rationally. The fewer directions they have to deal with the better. If too many people are telling the student to calm down or setting other parameters for release, the student will be confused.

If you are dealing with a one-on-one restraint situation, you are most likely the communicator. However, we have seen a team member standing to the side successfully fill the communicator role in scenarios involving both single and multiple restraints. Often the best communicator is the person who has the best rapport with the student.

The release decision

Have one team member make the decision to release the student. That person needs to be in contact with the student's body so he or she can judge the student's level of physical tension. Sometimes the student will profess to be calm while you still feel extreme tension in the body. This tension is a sign that the student is probably not ready to be released. It is very difficult for someone who is off to the side to recognize the physical cues signaling that a person is still potentially dangerous. If someone who is not in direct physical contact with the student assumes the communicator role, he or she should ask one of the restrainers whether or not the student is calm enough to be let up. If the student is released too soon and must be restrained again, the potential for injury is much greater.

It is important for team members to communicate clearly and trust one another's opinions during restraint interventions. If one person is not certain about letting a student up, there is probably a good reason for it.

Release parameters

The conditions or parameters for release can be as simple as requesting that the student be quiet for a minute. More extreme anger requires more elaborate steps. Regardless of the intensity, never talk to the student while he or she is yelling. Be patient. Once you sense that the student is listening, set the parameters.

If the situation involves multiple restraint, you can try taking the following steps:

1. Say, "If you are quiet and don't struggle for a minute, I will have those guys get off your legs."

2. Remind the student not to talk and encourage him or her to relax any physical tension during the 1-minute period. You can also coach the student through some deep breathing.

3. After the student has been quiet for a minute, have team members move off the legs but stay close by.

4. Set another parameter: "Let's try another minute of deep breathing, then we'll get off your arms and you can get up."

5. After the student has been quiet for the second minute and before you release him or her, establish what is to

happen next (e.g., the student will go to talk to the principal or school counselor). Make sure the student understands and agrees to this next step.

6. Release the student, but be cautious. The student could still be angry at you for the restraint.

Timed release

In some situations you may be able to release a student all at once—in other words, just let the student up. Some students realize right away that things have gotten out of hand, are embarrassed, and just want to get the situation over with. Other students are still angry. The restraint may make them more irate, but they are stable and also just want to cool down. If you release them, they will not attack you. Yet other students can be so enraged that they need a timed release. Releasing such students in increments allows them to get control of themselves gradually. Usually this is done in multiple restraint situations where there is a high level of aggression. The timed release can be short or long depending upon how angry the student is.

Escort Techniques

After you have separated the students and completed any restraint that may have been necessary, you will need to isolate the students from each other in order to interview them about their altercation. Most often the isolation area will be somewhere other than the fight location. To bring the student to the isolation area you have chosen requires some type of escort. In this section we will discuss five escort techniques. The first three are *controlled escorts*; the last two are *supervised escorts*.

In a controlled escort, a team member or members keep their hands on the student as he or she moves to the isolation area. If the student is too angry for you to use one of the forms of controlled escort, chances are you will need to restrain the student fully.

Supervised escorts are noncontact techniques. When using these techniques, you are not required to place your hands on the student at all. The student is calm enough that assertive verbal commands are sufficient to get him or her to go where you want. This does not mean that you simply send the student away unsupervised; students should never be left alone after a fight. Instead, you supervise the student within a *safety zone*, or out of the student's striking distance.

We have seen two or more teachers attempt an escort by carrying a student who is out of control. We have also seen a student accidentally get dropped and everyone involved in the situation fall at the same time. In general, carrying a student is very dangerous. If there is a fire or another emergency in which a student must be carried, then do it. But it may take up to four team members to perform a carry safely, and if the student is large the attempt will still be difficult. If the student is that much out of control, you should use a full restraint technique until he or she is calm. If the student will not calm down sufficiently, you should consider calling in the police and letting them handle the situation.

If the disputants involved are small—perhaps at the elementary level—a single staff member may be able to escort both safely. However, most escort situations will require at least one staff member per disputant, as the following techniques show.

Two-Person Backward Walk

The two-person backward walk requires two team members to escort the student. Most effective when the student is still angry but can be moved, the technique works particularly well after applying the Two-Person Arm Grab separation technique.

1. Two team members position themselves facing opposite the student, one on each side (Figure 31.1).

2. Each team member holds one of the student's lower or upper forearms in the outside hand and one of the student's upper arms in the crook of the inside arm.

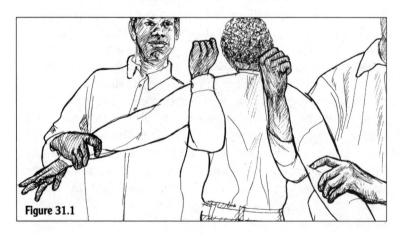

Figure 31.1

3. Once in this position, team members work together, walking forward at the same time (Figure 31.2). This causes the student to walk backward.

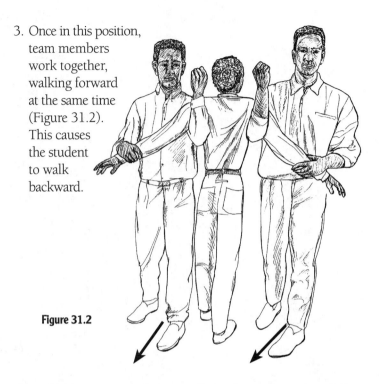

Figure 31.2

If you must move a student, it is always best to move him or her in a backward direction. Moving the student forward permits the student to resist you at every step—even change direction. Moving the student backward allows you to control the movement.

Double-Arm Walk

The Double-Arm Walk is a technique you can use when the student is calm enough to walk alone but is still angry enough that you feel some physical contact is needed. It is best applied when the student is too big for one team member to handle and you are concerned that he or she may try to continue to fight.

1. Both team members stay behind at a 45-degree angle and cautiously walk forward with the student (Figure 32.1).

2. As they do so, team members keep an outside hand on the student's shoulder and an inside hand on the student's upper arm or lower forearm.

3. If necessary, team members can initiate the Two-Person Backward Walk:

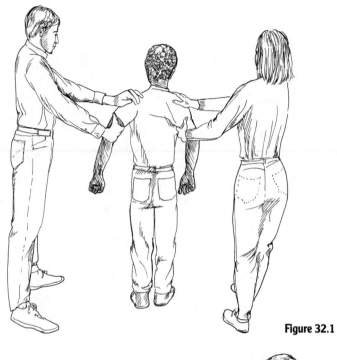

Figure 32.1

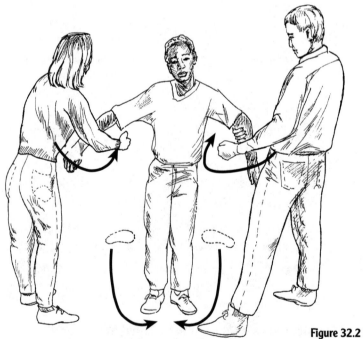

Figure 32.2

- Each team member steps with the outside foot toward the student (Figure 32.2).

- Each simultaneously takes his or her hand off the student's shoulder and hooks that arm underneath the student's arm.

- One team member remains stationary while the other person turns the student in the proper direction of travel (Figure 32.3).

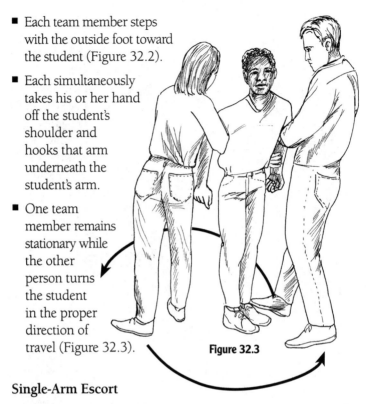

Figure 32.3

Single-Arm Escort

This technique is used when the student is generally under control and can be controlled by one person but still requires some physical management. Unfortunately, because you have only one of the student's hands under control, it is the technique in which you are most likely to be hit by an angry student. If you are hit, you probably misjudged the situation and should have used a two-person escort. Even though you can get hit using this technique, it is worth presenting because it is very common and, when done properly, can be effective.

1. Stand behind the student at a 45-degree angle.

2. Hold the student's upper arm with your inside hand (Figure 33.1). Keep your arm rigid and at a three-quarters extension to help prevent the student from swinging around and hitting you with the opposite hand.

3. Be prepared to push the student's arm forward if he or she starts to turn and swing at you (Figure 33.2). Pushing the arm forward as you let go prevents the student from turning toward you and getting in position to deliver a punch.

Figure 33.1

Figure 33.2

Single-Zone Escort

This form of supervised escort is appropriate when the student under escort is small enough that a single team member could restrain him or her if necessary.

1. Establish a safe distance between yourself and the student (Figure 34).

2. Maintain a 45-degree angle to the student; follow from behind for added security.

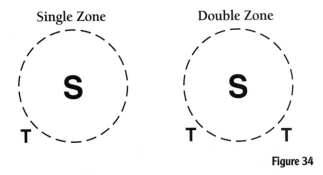

Figure 34

Double-Zone Escort

We advise using this form of supervised escort when the student is large enough that two team members would be required to provide any necessary restraint.

1. Both team members establish a safe distance from the student (Figure 34).

2. Both team members follow the student from behind at a 45-degree angle.

PERSONAL SAFETY

What do you do if you are attacked? In this section we will discuss some escape techniques and maneuvers to avoid incoming strikes. Beyond mastering these simple techniques, we recommend that you obtain further training in self-defense to protect yourself from possible attacks. Such skills may or may not be useful in specific classroom situations; however, they can boost your level of self-confidence, and that alone can be important in dealing with an aggressive student. The way you carry yourself is half the battle when it comes to personal defense. Having the assurance to speak with a clear, commanding, assertive tone will also help get you out of many physically threatening situations.

Prevention is the real key to ensuring your personal safety. Avoid situations where a student can attack you. Do not singlehandedly confront angry students or students whom you do not know if you can avoid doing so. Work as a team, and be aware of the context at all times. If despite your best efforts at prevention you find yourself attacked by a student, the following techniques may help you. After you have used any of these techniques, you can call for help or initiate a restraint, as appropriate.

Escape Techniques

If you find yourself attacked by a student, the escape techniques described in this section can help you. Escape techniques are most effective when used immediately. Don't hesitate if someone grabs you; if you do, escaping from an angry student's grasp will become that much more difficult.

Two of the variations described here involve the use of the Finger Release. Bending the fingers back in this approach results in some discomfort, thus causing the student to release the hold so you can effectively use your escape technique. Other, more extreme techniques exist and are commonly taught in self-defense courses. These maneuvers— stepping on a person's foot, hitting your heel into a shin, striking the groin area, and so forth—are intended to cause actual pain without necessarily causing injury. Using one of these more extreme techniques may be justifiable if it is the only way you can extricate yourself from a situation in which you are in danger of immediate physical harm. Even so, you should weigh the decision to use such techniques carefully: If your attempt fails, you may make your attacker even angrier, thus potentially making the situation worse.

Headlock

VARIATION A: FINGER RELEASE

1. Grab the student's small finger and ring finger and bend them backward (Figure 35).

2. Maintain this pressure as you step away from the student.

VARIATION B: PULL DOWN–PUSH UP RELEASE

In this maneuver, the leverage created protects the student's wrist from injury.

Figure 35

1. Turn your head toward the hand that is holding you (Figure 36.1).

2. Pull down on the student's wrist with one hand as you aggressively push up on the elbow with your other hand (Figure 36.2).

Figure 36.1

Figure 36.2

3. Step to the outside
   and slightly forward
   at an angle toward
   the student's elbow,
   twisting away
   from the hold
   (Figure 36.3).

Someone Grabs Your Tie

1. Pull back on your tie
   with one hand. This will
   take some pressure off
   your neck (Figure 37).

2. Grab the student's small
   finger and ring finger and
   bend them backward.

3. Simultaneously, keep
   your elbows up as high
   as you can to protect your face
   from potential strikes.

Figure 36.3

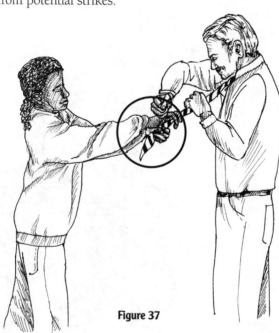

Figure 37

Alternatively, you can try putting the student in a bear hug (Figure 38). This will also prevent him or her from pulling on the tie. To avoid the whole problem, you could wear a clip-on or no tie at all.

Wrist Grabs

VARIATION A: CIRCULAR RELEASE

1. Step back, using the leg on the same side as the student's grab (Figure 39.1). Place the thumb of the grabbed hand under your palm and begin rotation clockwise.

Figure 38

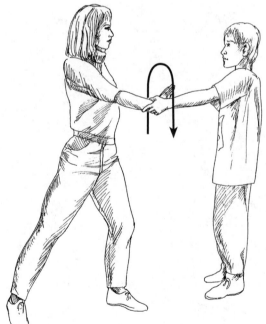

Figure 39.1

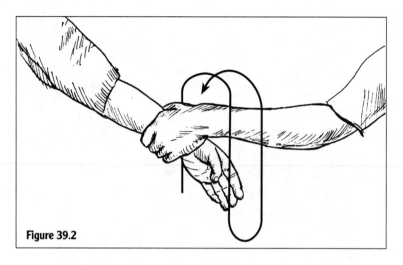

Figure 39.2

2. Complete the rotation of your arm and hand clockwise, then sharply reverse the direction to counterclockwise (Figure 39.2).

3. Pull back with your hand (Figure 39.3).

Figure 39.3

VARIATION B: FINGER RELEASE

1. Grab the student's small finger and ring finger and pull back until he or she releases the grip (Figure 40).

2. If the student does not release the hold while you are standing still, step forward with the foot on the opposite side as the grabbed hand, continuing to bend the student's fingers toward him or her.

Figure 40

Sustained Biting

VARIATION A: BITES ON THE HAND OR ARM

1. Push your hand or arm into the student's mouth with enough pressure to release the bite (Figure 41). The technique works because once you have pushed your arm far enough into the jaw, the mouth is unable to continue the biting motion.

2. Be careful not to push too hard. Too much pressure can cause the student's lip to split.

Figure 41

VARIATION B: BITES ELSEWHERE

1. Pinch the student's nostrils shut and hold them closed until the student stops biting (Figure 42). In this technique, the feeling of momentary restriction of air causes the student to stop biting.

2. Sometimes a student can bite you and still breathe through his or her mouth, thus rendering the pinching of the nostrils ineffective. If necessary, simultaneously push in with the part of your body that is being bitten.

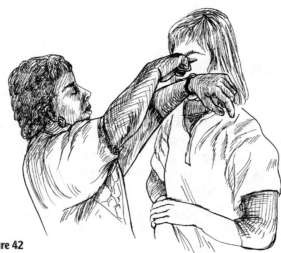

Figure 42

Bear Hugs

In a bear hug, someone grabs you from behind, pinning your arms (Figure 43.1). If a student gets you in a bear hug, try the following maneuver.

Figure 43.1

1. Jump and land with your feet in a wide stance parallel with each other (Figure 43.2).

Figure 43.2

205

2. As you land, thrust your buttocks into the person's upper thigh or lower hip area (Figure 43.3). Simultaneously grab your right wrist with your left hand and energetically raise your arms up and forward.

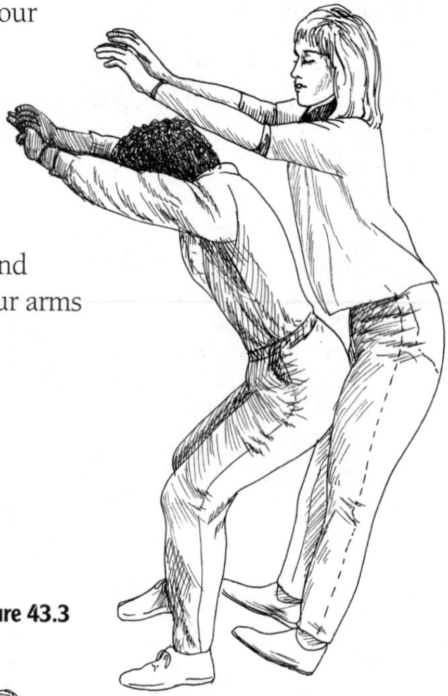

Figure 43.3

3. Duck your head underneath your right arm as you step forward with your left leg (Figure 43.4).

4. Pivot so that you are now facing the student, then step back again with your right leg.

Figure 43.4

Avoiding Incoming Strikes

Blocking and sidestepping techniques are among the more difficult skills to learn, and considerable practice will be necessary to master them. When developing skills to avoid strikes, you will need to learn how to anticipate when a strike is coming at you. A combatant's anger is a good indicator, as is the obvious charge or lunge toward you that often accompanies a strike. But more subtle physical indicators allow you to anticipate a strike even sooner. The most important of these indicators is hip movement. Good defensive fighters are able to anticipate an opponent's attack and time their defense with or before their opponent's movement. They do this by watching the total fighter and by focusing their attention on the hip region. It is difficult to move your arms or feet in an aggressive manner without moving your hips before you strike. As a result, hip movement indicates that someone is about to throw a punch.

In addition to hip movement, telegraphed movement is an important sign to watch for. Excess movement that occurs just before a punch is thrown, telegraphed movement could involve facial expressions of anger or stress. Often people will move or bite their lips before throwing a punch. Some will lean back and then swing. Others will look the other way, then strike. So look for telegraphed movement and be ready to react. You can practice recognizing telegraphing through this simple activity.

1. Two people face each other (Figure 44).

2. First person: Raise one hand with an open palm position. This hand becomes the target; keep it away from your face.

3. Second person: Make a fist with the hand opposite your forward leg. Stand reasonably close to the other person with your fist up. Try to hit the other person's open palm.

Figure 44

4. First person: Look for expressions or movements that signal when the punch is coming and try to move your hand out of the way before the punch is delivered.

5. Second person: Try not to show any expression or make any extra movements before punching.

The further away the puncher is, the easier it is to recognize movement. The closer the person, the more difficult.

Another factor to consider in blocking is the distance between you and the other person. If you anticipate being hit, you can step away to create more distance. The idea is that you are safer once you have put some distance between you and your attacker. Then if your block fails, the distance you have created gives you a second chance by making it less likely that the strike will hit you.

When sidestepping, you step to the side and slightly forward. You are still using the principle of creating distance between you and the attacker, but you are moving your body in a different direction. By sidestepping in this manner the distance you create gets you out of the striking zone. The technique of sidestepping is effective by itself for getting out of the way of strikes. When used in conjunction with a blocking technique, it is twice as effective.

In describing the following techniques, we will use clock reference points to describe direction; when interpreting these reference points, you can assume you are in the center of the clock before stepping.

Left Sidestep

The following instructions assume that you are sidestepping a straight punch directed at your face with the attacker's right hand.

Figure 45.1

1. Lean your head toward 10:30 (Figure 45.1). This will get your head out of the way.

2. Simultaneously shuffle to the left and slightly forward by pushing off with your right leg and stepping with the left to 10:30 in one quick motion. You should end up slightly to the side of and behind the punching arm (Figure 45.2).

Figure 45.2

Redirecting Block

1. Lean your head toward 10:30 and raise both hands in front of your face (Figure 46.1).

Figure 46.1

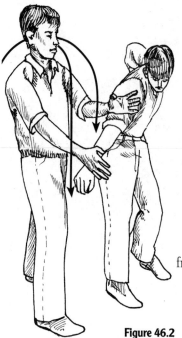

2. Extend your hands upward and sweep both arms in a circular motion to the right, redirecting the punch away from you (Figure 46.2).

3. Simultaneously shuffle to 10:30, as in Step 2 of the Left Sidestep. You should end up slightly behind the student.

Inward Block

This type of block protects you from a straight punch.

1. Step back with your right leg to 6:00 (Figure 47).

Figure 46.2

Figure 47

2. Bend your left arm at the elbow to a 90-degree angle.

3. Sweep your left arm toward the right and block, using the inside portion of the forearm. Your blocking arm will end up past your body.

Outward Block

This type of block protects you from a roundhouse swing, or a punch thrown from an outside position directed toward the side of your face.

1. Step back with your right leg to 6:00 (Figure 48.1).

2. Close your left fist and, bending your elbow at a 90-degree angle and starting from your left hip, rotate your arm counterclockwise.

Figure 48.1

3. Block the strike with your forearm. Your block should end up just past the left side of your head (Figure 48.2).

Figure 48.2

Upward Block

Use the upward block to protect against a strike to the top of your head.

1. Step back with your right leg to 6:00 (Figure 49).

2. Starting from the hip, close your left fist and bend your arm at the elbow at a 90-degree angle.

3. Bring your forearm straight up above your forehead to block the strike. Your forearm is the blocking surface.

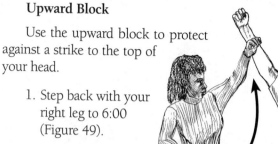

Figure 49

Downward Block

The downward block protects against kicks coming toward your groin area.

Figure 50.1

1. Step back with your right leg to 6:00 (Figure 50.1).

2. Bring your left hand with a closed fist to chin height.

3. Swing your arm down toward the strike, stopping the strike with your forearm (Figure 50.2).

Figure 50.2

Jamming/Smothering

An alternative to the use of blocking is the use of jamming and smothering techniques. In using these techniques you move in quickly on a student to prevent him or her from striking you. You do not execute any blocking or sidestepping motions. Instead, you get so close to the person that he or she cannot strike you. In effect, you have "jammed" or "smothered" the strike before it can build momentum. You know you have successfully jammed someone's punch when the person's arm is still bent and cannot extend out for the strike. Getting in this close means you will have to either restrain or push the person away from you immediately.

1. To effectively jam/smother a strike, position your body with your hip forward.

2. Keep your hands up to protect your face in case your attempt to jam/smother the strike fails.

3. Get inside the student's striking distance by pushing off with your rear leg and stepping forward with your front leg (Figure 51). This should be a quick, lunging motion.

4. Once inside, initiate a restraint or push the student away.

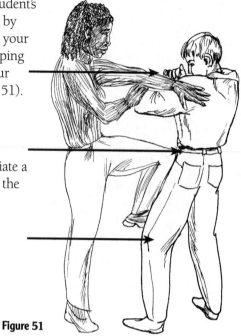

Figure 51

FIGHT KITS

What do you do when there is blood present in a fight? Today, blood has become a potentially deadly substance. We strongly recommend that if during your assessment of the situation you notice bleeding, you use a fight kit. You have heard of "safer sex"; using a fight kit is safer intervention. We have already established that you do not break up fights on impulse—you wait for help. Sometimes this means a fight may be in progress for a few seconds or so before you intervene. Your safety is important, and if that means letting the fight go until help arrives, you wait. If there is bleeding, you wait a little longer and break out the fight kit.

The purpose of a fight kit is to provide you with a degree of protection against blood-borne diseases. There are many, but the two of most concern are hepatitis B (serum hepatitis) and HIV (the AIDS virus). In the process of breaking up fights, you can sustain abrasions and scrapes. If infected blood comes in direct contact with these breaks in the skin, a blood-borne disease could be transmitted. It is important to put barriers between yourself and possibly contaminated blood. If you question this assertion, just ask yourself whether the school nurse or your local fire, rescue, or ambulance personnel expose their unprotected skin to someone else's blood. They do not; they follow universal precautions when dealing with blood. This means that they assume all blood is contaminated and treat it as such.

Your fight kit should contain the following materials:

- Latex gloves

- Plastic goggles

- Surgical masks

- Antiseptic wipes

- Spray bottle of 1/10 bleach-to-water solution

You would be surprised how fast you can get your fight kit out of a drawer and put on gloves, goggles, and mask—perhaps in under 30 seconds (Figure 52). Thirty seconds or so to provide potentially life-saving protection seems very worthwhile if the situation calls for it. It is best to put the gloves on first. Next put on the mask and the goggles, in that order. If you put the mask on after the goggles, the strap of the mask can get hung up on the goggles, knocking them off. In addition, having an established sequence with three easily remembered steps can save you time.

The antiseptic wipes and bleach solution are means to destroy viruses and bacteria. If you are not close to a place where you can effectively wash up, you can use these items. The antiseptic wipes are self-explanatory. You can mix the 1/10 bleach-to-water solution yourself and place it in a pump spray bottle. Simply mix 1 part bleach to 10 parts water. You can spray this solution on contaminated areas of skin and on clothing that you might not be able to remove immediately.

Figure 52

CROWD CONTROL

The control of an audience of fellow students at a fight scene varies in its demands and difficulty from school to school and fight to fight. In some schools, students listen and respond when teachers tell them to move on to class. In others, large crowds develop and become involved in the fight. In some cases crowds develop around a fight and become unruly when staff attempt to intervene; here the techniques used to break up the fight and not the fight itself are of concern to the crowd.

Even though it is difficult to predict crowd reactions to a given incident, containment will often be necessary. One step that will prove helpful to all containment efforts is to establish a recognizable and consistent approach in the school to deal with aggressive incidents. Students should be aware of the approach and perhaps have had a role in formulating it. The more familiar students are with your plan for managing fights, the more comfortable they will be with it and the less likely they will be to react impulsively at the scene of a fight.

Individuals on the team who are responsible for crowd control should follow these basic steps:

1. Try to form a perimeter around the fight scene.

2. Speak to gathering students in a nonthreatening but assertive tone. Make statements that reassure the crowd. For example:

   - "Everything is OK."
   - "You can help these people (the fighters) out by going to your class."
   - "Go to your rooms. Watching only makes them feel they have to fight more."

3. Be prepared to block students' paths or view if you are able.

4. Close corridor doors if possible to prevent more of a crowd from developing or to redirect hall traffic to other routes.

5. Be prepared to call for more assistance if needed.

DEALING WITH WEAPONS

- Knives
- Pens/pencils
- Screwdrivers
- Bats
- Guns
- Rocks
- Mace
- Bottles
- Large rings
- Two- and three-finger rings
- Staplers
- Padlocks
- Brass knuckles
- Metal nail files
- Heavy, fake gold chains
- Steelies (large ball bearings) in bag
- Belt-buckle knives
- Scissors
- Box cutters
- Stun guns
- Pen guns
- Slapjacks
- Auto batons
- Nunchakus
- Ammonia-filled spray bottles
- Weighted gloves
- Bayonets
- Perfume spray
- Compasses

This is a partial list of weapons that public school teachers have dealt with over the past few years. Although the list would appear to be comprehensive, students exhibit apparently endless creativity in adding new ones.

How do you deal with a weapon? The most effective way for an untrained, unarmored, unarmed person to deal with a weapon is to run. Under all circumstances you should choose flight over fight. If you choose to confront a student who has a weapon, chances are good that you will be hurt. But what if you are in a situation where you cannot get away or where another student is being injured? This question is difficult to answer categorically. However, we do have some practical suggestions for coping.

First, remain calm and try not to show fear. Showing fear signals that the student has control over you. If control is what the student is looking for, your showing fear can lead to his or her expressing the need for control by using the weapon on you. Try to maintain a confident posture and assertive tone. Tell the student to stop what he or she is doing and put the weapon down. At the same time, you might want to use your intercom system to call for help. If you cannot get to the intercom, yell.

If the student has a weapon that is not likely to be thrown, you can stay a safe distance away. However, if the student has something that may be hurled—a bottle, pipe, chair, stapler—staying out of range will be difficult. If you cannot leave the vicinity entirely, you can try the Jamming/Smothering technique described earlier. Moving inside the striking distance keeps the student from throwing the weapon at you. Staying on the outside only keeps you within the student's range.

If you are uncomfortable with the Jamming/Smothering strategy, you can try a shielding technique. This involves quick movement and a shield. Pick up a book, chair, table, or some other object that you can use as a shield against the strike. Quickly move toward the person and actively block the weapon with your shield. If you cannot block the weapon, you can maintain your position and block an attack if it comes by raising your shield as needed.

You can also try jamming with furniture. If, for example, there is a row of desks between you and the attacker, quickly push the desks into the person as hard as you can. The desks should jumble up and provide you with a brief time to escape, initiate restraint, or signal for assistance. This technique works best on tile or other smooth floors but can also be used with some success on carpeted areas.

After using one of these techniques, you may be able to escape or initiate a restraint. If you disarm the student, lock up the weapon or leave the scene with it. Make sure you do not freeze and allow the student to pick up something else to use as a weapon.

What if a student is injuring another student with a weapon? If you feel you can stop the aggression and not get hurt, then do so. If the fight involves swinging knives or gunfire, run for cover and call the police. We do not recommend putting your personal safety at risk to protect mutually consenting combatants. If one person is not a willing participant, the decision becomes more difficult. But in any case, the decision is a judgment call that only you can make.

PERIMETER AND AREA CONTROL

It is safe to say that most fights occur during arrival, dismissal, and transition times. When working together, you have to put your team where problems are most likely to occur. By doing so you are able to prevent fights from occurring or intervene before they become too involved. During transition times, we advise that you post yourselves outside in the hallways. This way you can mingle with students and look for trouble. You really cannot do this if you stay in your own room.

During arrival and dismissal times, a good procedure involves having willing team members divide up into two groups. One group stays in the building and works the hallways as usual. The other group handles the area outside the school building. The team members outside the building also divide into two groups—the perimeter and area teams. Members of the perimeter team spread themselves out along the edges of the dismissal area, whereas members of the area team disperse among the crowd of students. The perimeter team scan for trouble and alert the area team, who are positioned in the crowd and ready to intervene quickly if a fight breaks out. The perimeter team can then assist in the intervention or with crowd control. Perimeter and area team members can stay in communication by radio or by shouting.

If a fight does erupt during dismissal, a good crowd control technique to try is to have the school buses (if you have them) start beeping their horns and pulling away very slowly. Few students will want to miss the bus and walk home. Sometimes this strategy works; sometimes it does not.

Perimeter and area teams are also useful in cafeterias, as well as during outside breaks for lunch or recess. In a typical cafeteria you might position as few as two or three teachers in the corners or at doors. The area team might consist of one or two persons. The more people available the better, but the approach can be successful with just a few. It is possible to work with only a perimeter team or only an area team, but effectiveness will be reduced. It is best to have both.

A FINAL WORD

In this chapter we have described a number of techniques to maximize your safety and to minimize potential injury to both combatants and observing students. As we have stressed, physical intervention does not take the place of prevention, nor is it a substitute for a coherent and workable discipline code. However, when fights do take place, the knowledge and ability to intervene can help prevent unnecessary injuries. We therefore strongly urge that you learn these techniques well and practice them frequently—well in advance of the situations in which they will be needed.

Selected Resources on Effective Management of Student Aggression

The references annotated here provide useful, practical information on the prevention and reduction of student aggression. Together, they offer a wide variety of viewpoints and intervention techniques. Teachers and other school personnel are urged to selectively consult these sources as the needs of their own schools, classrooms, and students suggest.

Apter, S. J. (1982). *Troubled children, troubled systems.* New York: Pergamon.

As the author states, "The purpose of this book is to demonstrate the utility of an ecological approach to troubled children." The focus is on means for altering the significant systems—education, family, mental health—that impact upon disturbed and disturbing youth. The coordination and comprehensiveness of services rendered to youth by such sources are stressed, as is the importance of a dual emphasis on both direct (to the youth) and indirect (to servicegivers) intervention and consultation.

Casserly, M. D., Bass, S. A., & Garrett, J. R. (1980). *School vandalism: Strategies for prevention.* Lexington, MA: Lexington.

This book provides a thorough discussion of the school vandalism problem in the United States, including its scope and forms, targets and trends, who the primary vandals are, and what to do about it. A number of alternative prevention and intervention programs are described and illustrated, including those focused upon building security, target hardening, architectural design, offender accountability, behavior modification, community relations, curriculum innovation, and more. In all, this resource is a sound, comprehensive statement of the problem and its possible remediation.

Charles, C.M. (1992). *Building classroom discipline* (4th ed.). New York: Longman.

Charles presents here an overview of eight prominent models of classroom discipline. Each model's central ideas are described, along with its key intervention procedures and exercises illustrating its use. Examined are (a) Redl's psychodynamic approach, employing self-control, situational assistance, and reality appraisal techniques; (b) Kounin's emphasis on effective lesson management via teacher "with-it-ness," skilled management of lesson movement, group focus, and situation avoidance; (c) Skinner's contingency management stance, involving the modification of behavior by means of judicious presentation and withholding of reinforcers contingent upon, respectively, the enactment of desirable and undesirable behaviors; (d) Ginott's congruent communication model, relying on a focus upon student behavior, the avoidance of labeling, the acknowledgment of feelings, and the use of cooperation invitations; (d) Dreikurs' goal confrontation approach, concerned with correcting the content of students' attention, power, and revenge-seeking goal behaviors; (e) Jones' concern with enhancing student self-control by teacher employment of effective body language, incentive systems, and individualized assistance; (f) Canter's assertive discipline and its use of appropriate behavioral expectations and limit settings; and (g) Glasser's control theory perspective, concretized by teachers functioning as "lead-managers" who stimulate and encourage, rather than "boss-managers" who dictate student behavior.

Christenson, S., & Conoley, J.C. (Eds.). (1992). *Home-school collaboration*. Silver Springs, MD: National Association of School Psychologists.

Christenson and Conoley provide an especially comprehensive consideration of a wide variety of existing and potential avenues for facilitative collaboration between school personnel and students' family members. Theory, research, and practice are explored as the authors suggest effective means for better understanding and more fruitfully promoting such collaboration. Obstacles to the success of collaborative attempts are identified, and ways to overcome those obstacles are proposed for students both with and without special needs.

Cohen, H.L., Schaefer, C.E., & Cohen, J.J. (1980). *Therapies for school behavior problems.* San Francisco: Jossey-Bass.

Wide-ranging and eclectic, this handbook provides brief descriptions of relevant interventions for an array of school behavior problems, several including aggression as a significant component. Thus, for example, for the problem of aggressive peer relationships, approaches described include psychosituational classroom intervention, self-control training, classical conditioning, time-out, and a series of punishment techniques. For the problem of disrespect and defiance toward the teacher, solutions offered include transactional analysis, family therapy, self-control training, special classes, and the use of alternative schools.

Emmer, E.T., Evertson, C.M., Sanford, J.P., Clements, B.S., & Worsham, M.E. (1984). *Classroom management for secondary teachers.* Englewood Cliffs, NJ: Prentice-Hall.

Evertson, C.M., Emmer, E.T., Clements, B.S., Sanford, J.P., & Worsham, M.E. (1984). *Classroom management for elementary teachers.* Englewood Cliffs, NJ: Prentice-Hall.

These highly practical resources for elementary and secondary school teachers deal with classroom organization, arrangement, and materials; classroom rules and procedures; the management of student work; the use of rewards and penalties; activity planning; behavior management techniques; and the needs of special student groups.

Gagne, E.E. (1982). *School behavior and school discipline.* Lanham, MD: University Press of America.

Gagne examines school disciplinary practices via consideration of such variables as school climate, peer expectations, and the role of formal and informal grouping arrangements in the management of deviance. Specific types of disciplinary interventions described and promoted include (a) narrowing boundaries; (b) creating orderliness, meaningfulness, and predictability in the classroom; (c) lowering student tension and frustration levels; (d) clarifying reference group expectations; (e) encouraging acknowledgment of and respect for differences; and (f) employing behavior modification techniques. Also provided is a useful discussion of the legal aspects of various disciplinary practices.

Gangs, guns, and kids. (1992). *Journal of Emotional & Behavioral Problems, Spring, 1*(1).

This whole issue is devoted to youth gangs and their school and community impact. Discussed are such topics as gang identifiers and terminology, conduct-disordered gang members, cults as gangs, gang-related shooting incidents, school searches, and gang intervention programming.

Gaustad, J. (1991). Schools respond to gangs and violence. *Oregon School Study Council Bulletin, 34*(9).

This whole issue traces the developing scope of the gang problem in United States schools, giving special attention to violence, guns, and drugs. A brief survey of countersteps taken in a sample of school districts is outlined. The violence prevention strategies examined include prosocial skills training, gang awareness curricula, parent involvement programming, and job training opportunities for high-risk youth.

Goldstein, A. P. (1988). *The Prepare Curriculum: Teaching prosocial competencies.* Champaign, IL: Research Press.

This multicomponent psychoeducational curriculum has been designed to teach a broad array of prosocial competencies to aggressive youth. For each of its 10 independent segments, relevant theory and research are described. The major focus, however, is on course-length intervention plans for each segment: (a) problem-solving training, (b) interpersonal skills training, (c) situational perception training, (d) anger control training, (e) moral reasoning training, (f) stress management training,

(g) empathy training, (h) recruiting supportive models, (i) cooperation training, and (j) understanding and using groups. To aid in curriculum delivery, a full discussion is provided regarding student motivation, classroom management, and generalization of gain.

Goldstein, A. P., & Glick, B. (1987). *Aggression Replacement Training: A comprehensive intervention for aggressive youth.* Champaign, IL: Research Press.

Aggression Replacement Training is designed to teach youths alternatives to aggressive and antisocial behaviors. It has three components: prosocial skills training, designed to teach a 50-skill curriculum of prosocial behaviors; anger management, implemented to teach youths how to control their own response to anger; and moral reasoning, intended to help youths think about moral dilemmas in a less egocentric, more principled manner. In addition to detailed descriptions of these procedures, the book describes supportive research and provides relevant forms and materials, as well as guidelines for program administration.

Goldstein, A. P., Harootunian, B., & Conoley, J. C. (1994). *Student aggression: Prevention, control and replacement.* New York: Guilford.

This volume begins with a thorough discussion of school violence in the United States—levels, types, locations, causes, and correlates. The book is primarily an application-oriented, detailed description of research-based interventions designed to prevent, reduce, and substitute other behaviors for student aggression. Interventions at the student, peer, teacher, school, family, and community levels are described and examined, in the belief that all such levels must be addressed for enduring student change to occur.

Goldstein, A. P., & Rosenbaum, A. (1982). *Aggress-less.* Englewood Cliffs, NJ: Prentice-Hall.

This self-help book presents an array of aggression reduction techniques and aggression alternatives. Described in a step-by-step manner are procedures for relaxation, self-control, calming others, constructive communication, negotiation, contracting, use of rewards and nonaggressive punishments, prosocial skill building, and assertiveness training.

Greenbaum, S., Turner, B., & Stephens, R. D. (1989). *Set straight on bullies*. Malibu, CA: National School Safety Center.

The authors offer a comprehensive overview of the problem of bullying in United States schools. The likely frequency and dispersion of bullying are described, as are salient characteristics of bullies and their typical victims. A series of prevention and intervention strategies are offered, highlighting the degree to which solutions are the responsibility not only of school personnel but also of parents and the general public.

Hyman, J. A., & Wise, J. H. (Eds.). (1979). *Corporal punishment in American education*. Philadelphia: Temple University Press.

This comprehensive volume of contributed articles deals with the use and abuse of corporal punishment. Discussed are the history of the use of corporal punishment; its support in tradition, law, and public opinion; case studies buttressing pleas for its elimination; consideration of research evaluating its effectiveness; and disciplinary procedures that might function as viable alternatives for altering student behavior.

Kauffman, J. M., Hallahan, D. P., Mostert, M. P., Trent, S. C., & Nuttycombe, D. G. (1993). *Managing classroom behavior*. Boston: Allyn & Bacon.

This behaviorally oriented, teacher-friendly text offers concrete suggestions for altering disruptive and noncompliant student behavior. Substantial emphasis is placed on the importance of the teacher-student relationship, the use of classroom peers, teacher-teacher collaboration, and the roles of parents in the behavior change effort. Case examples illustrate main points.

Knopf, H. M. (1987). School based intervention for discipline problems. In C. A. Maher (Ed.), *Psychoeducational intervention in schools*. Needham Heights, MA: Allyn & Bacon.

Knopf's chapter provides a summary overview of the conclusions that may appropriately be drawn from research on school discipline practices. Stressed first is the need for understanding of the social and developmental roots of the behavior for which discipline is planned. Primary, secondary, and tertiary intervention procedures are briefly examined, with emphasis upon those relative few whose effectiveness has been supported by evaluation research. These include (a) rule specification, practice, and monitoring; (b) teacher "with-it-ness"; (c) teacher attentiveness and intervention preparedness; (d) teacher facilitation of participation and pacing; (e) social skills training; and (f) effective use of teacher praise.

Kodluboy, D. W., & Evenrud, L. A. (1993). School-based interventions: Best practices and critical issues. In A. P. Goldstein & C. R. Huff (Eds.), *The gang intervention handbook*. Champaign, IL: Research Press.

Kodluboy and Evenrud provide a broad discussion of gangs in United States schools. They discuss gangs' incidence, recruitment and motivation for joining, resultant problem behaviors, and the impact of gangs on schools. The school climate and academic and home-school instructional practices are described and evaluated. The authors also identify a literature-based "best practice" approach as particularly effective in responding to a perceived gang problem. Especially valuable is the presentation of guidelines by which to predict the success of transferring a "best practice" to a new context.

Lewis, R. (1991). *The discipline dilemma*. Victoria: The Australian Council for Educational Research.

Lewis provides a thorough description and illustration of three different styles of classroom discipline: student-oriented, teacher-oriented, and group-oriented. The concrete utilization and advantages and disadvantages of each are examined. Especially useful is the manner in which these contrasting approaches to classroom discipline are related to important qualities of the context in which they are used. Contextual considerations include student characteristics (e.g., age, developmental level), teacher characteristics (e.g., stress level, preferred teaching techniques), and characteristics of the school itself (e.g., prevailing discipline philosophy and policy). A useful added feature is the brief description of how, and under what classroom circumstances, the three disciplinary styles might be effectively combined.

McGinnis, E., & Goldstein, A. P. (1984). *Skillstreaming the elementary school child: A guide for teaching prosocial skills*. Champaign, IL: Research Press.

Goldstein, A. P., Sprafkin, R. P., Gershaw, N. J., & Klein, P. (1980). *Skillstreaming the adolescent: A structured learning approach to teaching prosocial skills.* Champaign, IL: Research Press.

These two volumes present a step-by-step description of the Skillstreaming approach to social skills training. In this approach, skills are taught via (a) modeling, which demonstrates how to use the behaviors constituting the skill; (b) role-playing, which provides guided opportunities to rehearse these competent behaviors; (c) performance feedback, which provides praise or reinstruction following role-playing; and (d) generalization training, which encourages the transfer and maintenance of newly learned skills through homework assignments and other techniques. Skills covered in the book for adolescents fall into six categories: beginning social skills, advanced social skills, skills for dealing with feelings, skill alternatives to aggression, skills for dealing with stress, and planning skills. Those in the book for elementary-age students are grouped as follows: classroom survival skills, friendship-making skills, skills for dealing with feelings, skill alternatives to aggression, and skills for dealing with stress.

Munthe, E., & Roland, E. (1989). *Bullying: An international perspective.* London: David Fulton.

Part 1 of this book provides an overview of the nature and scope of bullying behavior in schools in a series of Western nations. Discussed are definitions, incidence statistics, typical school and community settings in which bullying occurs, and perpetrator and victim characteristics. Part 2 is intervention-oriented, again with an international perspective. Described and illustrated are a number of procedures to alter the bullying behavior of perpetrators or the responses to bullying by victims. Interventions such as vigilant supervision, the cooperative classroom, social education curricula, a tutoring model, victim empowerment, parent and community involvement, and packaged approaches (e.g., Kidscape and the Common Concern Method) are examined.

National School Safety Center. (1990). *Gangs in schools.* Malibu, CA: Author.

This pamphlet describes the growing presence and impact of youth gangs in United States schools. The special features of various ethnic gangs are depicted. Diverse prevention and intervention programs are examined, and a variety of school and community resources responsible for such programming are identified.

O'Callaghan, J. B. (1993). *School-based collaboration with families: Constructing family-school-agency partnerships that work.* San Francisco: Jossey-Bass.

This source's purpose is captured well by its subtitle. Such partnerships, one is told, may be built effectively by the "ecosystem consultant," whose energies are devoted to organizational restructuring, inservice training, family-oriented intervention, and related attempts to alter the school context in which aggressive youths function. Particular procedural emphasis is placed on constructing collaborative participation among and between such ecosystem components.

O'Leary, K. D., & O'Leary, S. G. (1977). *Classroom management: The successful use of behavior modification.* New York: Pergamon.

This volume is a compilation of primarily applied, "how-to" articles. It describes the effective classroom use of teacher attention, modeling, and token reinforcement programs, as well as punishment techniques, self-management procedures, the use of peers as change agents, and related behavioral interventions.

Olweus, D. (1978). *Aggression in the schools: Bullies and whipping boys.* Washington, DC: Hemisphere.

This report is of a major research and intervention program concerned with the problem of bullying in schools. Though the report pertains to Scandinavia, its implications for United States schools are substantial. The types of youngsters most prone to becoming either bullies or whipping boys are described, as are the classroom and school contexts in which such aggressive behaviors are most likely to occur. Useful remedial measures are also presented.

Stephens, R. D. (1993). School-based interventions: Safety and security. In A. P. Goldstein & C. R. Huff (Eds.), *The gang intervention handbook.* Champaign, IL: Research Press.

This survey of school-based assessment and intervention approaches helps educators identify the level of gang activity in a given school or school district, then intervene to prevent or remove such influences. Prevention and intervention techniques described include a gang prevention curriculum, clear behavioral expectations for students, a formal dress code, graffiti removal, a gang crime reporting hot line, victim protection programming, a visitor screening policy, parent gang-awareness training, parent and community involvement in security efforts, cooperation with law enforcement, and more.

Walker, H. M. (1979). *The acting-out child: Coping with classroom disruption.* Boston: Allyn & Bacon.

Walker gives here an especially thorough and user-friendly presentation of behavior modification techniques as applied to student aggression. The acting-out child's typical behaviors are described in detail. Interventions include the establishment and use of classroom rules, procedures for observing and recording student classroom behavior, and a full array of behavior management techniques. Illustrative case studies facilitate actual classroom use. Also described are techniques for involving parents in the behavior change effort and means for promoting generalization of gain.

Walker, J. E. (1990). *Behavior management: Practical approach for educators* (5th ed.). Columbus, OH: Merrill.

This book is, in part, a straightforward, "how-to" presentation of basic behavior modification procedures as applied in school contexts. Thus, principles of reinforcement, reinforcer identification, and behavioral methods for both increasing desirable behaviors (e.g., shaping, contingency contracting) and decreasing undesirable behaviors (e.g., extinction, time-out) are considered in detail. In addition, this comprehensive volume examines a series of psychodynamic, environmental, and home-based interventions—each designed to alter inappropriate student behaviors and replace them with appropriate alternatives.

Wielkiewicz, R. M. (1986). *Behavior management in the schools.* Needham Heights, MA: Pergamon.

This volume offers a thorough presentation of principles and practice in the use of behavioral techniques to alter student aggression and other disruptive or inappropriate behaviors. Useful assessment procedures and steps for facilitating home-school collaboration are also provided.

Index

233

About the Authors

Arnold P. Goldstein joined the clinical psychology section of Syracuse University's Psychology Department in 1963 and both taught there and directed its Psychotherapy Center until 1980. In 1981, he founded the Center for Research on Aggression, which he currently directs. He joined Syracuse University's Division of Special Education in 1985 and in 1990 helped organize and codirect the New York State Task Force on Juvenile Gangs. Dr. Goldstein has a career-long interest, as both researcher and practitioner, in difficult-to-reach clients. Since 1980, his main research and psychoeducational focus has been youth violence. He is the developer of psychoeducational programs and curricula designed to teach prosocial behaviors to chronically antisocial persons. Dr. Goldstein's many books include, among others, *Skillstreaming the Adolescent: A Structured Learning Approach to Teaching Prosocial Skills; Aggression Replacement Training: A Comprehensive Intervention for Aggressive Youth; The Prepare Curriculum: Teaching Prosocial Competencies; Refusal Skills: Preventing Drug Use in Adolescents; Delinquents on Delinquency;* and *The Gang Intervention Handbook.*

James Palumbo has been a special education teacher in the Syracuse, New York, city school district for the last 8 years. He received his undergraduate and master's degrees in education from Syracuse University. He currently holds a third-degree black belt at Syracuse Kenpo Jutsu Karate. For the past 10 years he has been an adjunct instructor for Syracuse University's Physical Education Department, where he teaches women's self-defense and karate. When not teaching, he actively pursues mountaineering, rock/ice climbing, mountain bike racing, salmon fishing, and cross-country skiing.

Susan Striepling holds a master's degree in education and has for many years been a social studies and reading teacher in challenging middle school contexts. She currently serves as an education consultant and trainer at the national level. Her major areas of professional concern include classroom management, home-school collaboration, and alternative curriculum delivery systems.

Anne Marie Voutsinas is currently a teacher on special assignment with the Syracuse, New York, city schools. Her current responsibilities are in staff development, especially in the areas of cooperative learning, classroom management, integration of curriculum, assessment, and mentoring of new educators. Her classroom experience includes many years in a middle school setting, primarily in a mathematics-science magnet program. She is the mother of three children, a former cub scout leader, and a member of the Board of Directors of the Syracuse Teachers Association.